—

Lost & Found

Finding The Power In Your Voice

The creative journey of one Black woman
finding her voice to tell her story.

PYENG THREADGILL

Lost and Found, Finding the Power in Your Voice / Pyeng Threadgill —1st ed.

Hardcover: 978-1-9569893-1-1

DEDICATION

To my teachers
and my original dream team, Nikolai and Luna.

CONTENTS

AN INVITATION TO READERS

I began writing this book three years ago, in 2020, during the early months of the pandemic. It began as short musings, which I often shared on social media, and as newsletters, and I eventually realized it could be expanded into a greater volume. For many months, while so many of us were trapped indoors—witnessing the ravages of COVID-19, a diseased political system, and growing uprisings—writing became a refuge and sanctuary for me. I hope this book gives you the opportunity to both hear yourself and find, or follow, your voice. I hope you find time and space in which to read that allows you to feel liberated, refreshed, and inspired. Put your feet up, stretch your legs out, prepare a hot beverage. Sit at a cafe, in a cozy hammock, on your porch, or in a favorite chair. Perhaps you'll choose to read in a waiting room, on a train, or settled by the ocean. Notice if your mind wanders and what it wonders about. Turn off your phone and see what comes to the surface.

INTRODUCTION

Many years ago, I started studying Somatic Voicework™ The LoVetri Method with the method's founder, Jeanie LoVetri. At the time, I had a fairly successful music career considering that I was an independent artist. I had two recorded albums, a record label, a booking agent, a child, and a husband—and I wasn't yet 30.

I started studying with Jeanie when my husband and I still lived in Northern California. A fellow singer/songwriter, Jamie Leonhart, had referred me to her work, and I felt called to her method of including the body and using voice science. At that time, I would regularly make trips back to New York to perform with my New York-based band, to feed my artistic hunger, and feel the charge of the city, always returning back to California living. The slower pace of the Bay Area was a good match for being both newly married and a new mother. I had a whole host of new responsibilities, which overwhelmed me. The morning routine, alone—of getting showered, dressed, nursing my daughter, preparing breakfast, my husband and I both having to make our way to school— was enough to leave me slightly sweaty and exasperated by the time I arrived at class for my Alexander Technique teacher training.

When I began working with Jeanie, I was somewhere between my second and third album, and near completion of my certification as a teacher of the Alexander Technique. Yet, despite all the outward success of my life, I was having real trouble with my voice. It wasn't something that I wanted advertised, but those close to me knew that I would sometimes lose my voice.

Anyone who has ever lost their voice, particularly a performer, knows that this can be an *extremely* stressful experience. What perhaps begins as a fun, "Hey, check out my sexy, sultry sound!" turns to, "Okay, when is this going to end?" to a panicked, "What I am going to fucking do?! My career is over!"

Of course, non-singers rarely worry about the sound of their voice or vocal health. Elementary school teachers, dance instructors, radio and talk show hosts, podcasters, and motivational speakers all rely heavily on their voices and can often become hoarse or vocally fatigued, yet they remain unphased. However, as a singer, not having access to the full range of your voice feels like being trapped in a straightjacket or lost in a maze.

Fortunately, it was at this point that I met Jeanie. I had taken the first level of her teacher training in Somatic Voicework when, as luck would have it, I had laryngitis. Over an entire weekend, I was meeting and interacting with new people in my field using my raspy, squawking voice. I felt complete embarrassment at that being their first impression of me. My voice eventually came back, but this pattern of coming and going—my voice acting as an apparition—had been repeating itself for years.

At one point, in the midst of winter, my band and I had a residency at the long-standing downtown music venue, Nublu. I sang with a head cold through an amp that was too low, while my bandmates' amps were ultra-high. (Note to all singers: Always be sure to turn up your volume when performing live—your voice can't compete with electric instruments and live drums.) That was the vibe at Nublu, and much of what I loved. But that night, and the next day, my voice continued to be hoarse. I was accustomed to being hoarse after a late night of performing and hanging out with friends, but the next day my voice felt strained. It was hard to speak, and when I did, it felt like someone had shoved another person's head over mine—like I was being forced to disguise myself. I didn't realize it at the time, but I had lost my voice that night, and it would take more than a year to heal and retrain my instrument.

Several days went by, then weeks, and more weeks—yet, my voice never fully returned. I knew something was wrong when I found it easier *not* to talk to my friends and family, since speaking had become physically exhausting. Singing wasn't an option. I could force out some low pitches, but if I tried to hit notes in my higher range, my voice would turn into a breathy, whistle tone, or worse—no sound at all.

Eventually, I made an appointment with a throat specialist. After viewing my vocal folds, the specialist informed me that they were extremely swollen. There was no pathology—such as a polyp or node—but had I not been careful in how I approached singing, I could have developed one. The swelling was producing the unpredictable breathiness and raspy tone. The message was clear: the more I continued to sing in my usual manner, the more my vocal folds would continue to be irritated. I was devastated.

The doctor recommended I see a voice teacher and speech therapist to start retraining my singing voice. What commenced was months of howling and hooting, stretching my tongue out, and watching myself in the mirror as I made sound. I was committed to my practice, and at the same time, I felt completely in the dark as to how my voice would improve. I would make some progress and then fall back. Nonetheless, I was super determined, yet also panicked, because I had a summer tour lined up and a new album to record.

My band members were depending on me, and I had even higher expectations of myself. Willpower saw me through all these events. I held a live recording performance in Williamsburg; toured in Italy, France, and Spain as a headlining artist at a slew of awesome jazz and blues festivals; ate delicious food; lived well; and when I returned home, I recorded an album of my own music.

Despite accomplishing these things, I realized that my voice still wasn't back to normal. It was important to me to push through touring and recording, but eventually I felt it was time to see Jeanie in order to figure out what was going on with my voice. I had already done some work to help solve some technical problems with my voice, but I knew there was something more—that deeper layer of emotion.

I felt it intuitively—in my marriage, in the challenges of being a young mother, in trying to hold onto my career as a performer, and even in my relationship to singing and performing. In the entire time I had been learning various vocal warmups, my former teacher never once asked how I was doing (*like, really doing*). She kept our communication on the surface—technical and determined, yet friendly. Deep down, I was scared—scared that my voice wouldn't get better, scared that I would lose my connection to music, scared of the fragility of my relationship, and scared because a part of me felt like it would disappear.

When I reconnected with Jeanie, it became clear to me that I was ready to go all in this time. Although I had a level 1 certification in Somatic Voicework™, I hadn't really explored it deeply. Returning to work with her, I felt ready not only to connect with the technical aspects of my vocal training, but also to the emotional and spiritual.

I began seeing Jeanie on a regular basis. With some income from teaching, and the support of my husband, I was able to invest in consistent lessons. In Jeanie's studio, I immediately noticed how encouraged and appreciated I felt, regardless of what sounds I made. Jeanie didn't ask me to do wild vocal acrobatics or judge me; she simply listened and guided me. When I knew I wanted more out of my voice, and even when I could tell she was working to help my voice release in a bigger way—she never became impatient or seemed preoccupied. Jeanie was always right by my side on the journey—just "waiting for the bus," as she likes to tell us. And steadily, the bus arrived.

What made working with Jeanie so different was that she never asked for my voice to be something that it wasn't. I wasn't asked to create a forced vibrato, as I had been in college, nor to make my voice louder, as I had been by my former teacher. Jeanie asked me to sing notes easily and comfortably, and whatever came out—that was my voice. If my voice was ever slightly stuck, there was a logical reason, and she was more than willing to wait for that part of my instrument to become unstuck. Whether my voice was loud and boisterous, or light and delicate—that was natural, too. Her willingness and patience made me willing and patient with myself, and therefore, curious—as curious and interested as I sensed she was.

There was a whole world inside me! Who or what had made me think that it was unrecoverable?! I was born into this, and music had always been my close friend. Jeanie both taught me and gifted me with the awareness that singing, in all parts of my range, could be free and fun, ridiculous and pleasurable, just as it had been when I was young. She enabled me to truly *enjoy* vocalizing. Unlike my days in the practice rooms of Oberlin, I now wanted to linger on vocal warmups. Practicing wasn't just about singing "well" or "pretty," and it wasn't about punishing myself, either. Practicing helped me to better understand myself and what was happening inside this mysterious and intricate instrument.

But also, Jeanie brought heart to her teaching, along with a deep empathy and love for teaching, and honoring people's humanity in general. Because she worked so steadily, and without judgment, it allowed me to feel. In some ways, those months of retraining helped me to further access my ability to listen more deeply to my voice, sound, and its messages. Prior to my album and touring, and ever since my voice had been injured, I was too scared to fully feel. I was afraid that if I allowed myself to feel, I would crack—not just my voice, but ME!

When I went to study with Jeanie for the second time, I knew I was ready to allow my heart, not just my voice, to become open, to be messy, fearful, tearful, and anything else that would emerge. I knew that holding back all those emotions had been affecting my vocal recovery and that singing, like always, would bring me back home.

Now, when students come to my studio, I always remember the love, kindness, and safety that Jeanie gave to me. Even though I no longer see her very often, I believe the love that she teaches with is imbued in her method. While it is functional voice training, at the core of her technique is teaching with heart. What other way would anyone want to sing?

Your Intuitive Voice

Clearing

Following Inspiration

VOICE LOG #44

If I just keep trusting my instincts, I think it'll be alright.

WHOSE VOICE IS THIS?

There's this part of you—you hear it walking through the house, going to the store, making your way to work. You hear it riding on the subway or driving in your car. There's this voice in your head which leaps, crawls, saunters, or barks out of your mouth.

Inside your head, it has one shape—it has a height and depth you've always known and grown accustomed to hearing out loud. Yet, when you play back recordings of yourself on videos, or listen to phone messages, you wonder, "whose voice is this?" It's the same voice that you use to sing along to your favorite songs while driving down the freeway, dancing at your friend's birthday party, or when home alone.

All over the world, composers, painters, sculptors, dancers, playwrights, and other artists sequester themselves in rooms—alone or with like-minded folk—to call on this voice. They sit at pianos, stand in front of blank canvas, and balance on Marley in order to draft an artistic impulse or impression—something they saw in their head, felt in their heart, or heard in their mind.

Ever since I was a little girl, I have been humming and singing to myself—making up songs, talking to my toys and stuffed animals, singing my heart out to *Annie*, and living in a world of make believe. I was like Alice in Wonderland, following my imaginary rabbit friend into the different portals, bridges, and tunnels of both my mind and the world around me. I was an only child and very happy. I felt safe and loved with my mom and my dad, in our little nest.

I grew up in a one-bedroom apartment of a 6-floor tenement building on the Lower East Side of New York City. With the comfort of my imagination, and my mom, things felt cozy in our community of spiked-hair punks, drunks, neighborhood homeless people, jazz-talking musicians, dancers, and artists who spoke and lived by their own special code. Being a child in this kind of environment constantly fed my voice and creativity—so much so that my mother had to devise a secret language to prevent me from talking to anyone and everyone I saw on the street.

I grew up in the former Lower East Side of New York, now known as the East Village, in the 1980s, when the body of every subway car was tattooed with graffitti, before Tompkins Square Park and Washington Square Park had curfews like teenagers, and before yoga and health food stores were a fashion statement. My breeding ground was a walk-through museum where I would pass the time roller skating, climbing over cement sculptures on the playground, and racing my friend, Alexander. Time flew by and ideas came to me without force.

I imagined a world where kids could drive their own cars, side by side with adults, and attempted to meet this demand by constructing them out of broken laundry carts, pieces of metal, wood, and cardboard. I sang to myself at the Tompkins Square Library and in its gallery, which was founded by my mom. I sang in the community gardens where my mom and her friends, like Teresa, Zoe, or Sophie, would plant and till soil in order to grow something fresh and new in this evolving downtown scene of New York City.

I wrote and recorded songs on my cassette tape recorder as my parents' friends cheered me on. And although I documented it on tape, I didn't have to search to find my voice because my voice was leading me. My voice was drawing itself all over the walls of my room and echoing down the hallways of our apartment building. It was drifting out of our front windows that opened out onto East 6th Street. It was sitting on the fire escape and rushing up the stairwell to find my friend, Cavana, at her house on East 13th. My voice was telling me where to go. Just like Alice in Wonderland, messages were being left for me in random places suggesting, "sing me," "write me," and "record me"—and so, I would willingly follow. This was the gift of my childhood and the community

I grew up in.

The adults who my parents worked with and were close to invested a large portion of their time into playing, in order to continuously source new and fresh ideas. It was non-negotiable. It was actually a way of life, a means of communication, spiritual transmission, and transportation. This language, known as music and dance, was natural to me. When I wasn't trying, a voice would come out on its own—a voice with its own strut, temperature, and timing.

However, as I grew up, it would become harder to trust my voice and my musical instincts. Without the closeness of community I experienced growing up, like landmarks in a forest, I felt lost and lacking in confidence. I felt farther away from my tribe. And as I grew older, I would begin to question the validity of my footsteps, especially when I saw myself veering from the path I had expected to take.

Over time, I began to discover that the path to finding your voice often becomes a process of following. The writing on the bottles would change from "sing me," "write me," and "record me" to new things like "rest," "listen," "trust," and "now sing." And, if you lean in and heed the call, *your music* will start to come through, allowing your voice to lead as it has always wanted to do.

NO FILTER

No filter
No screen
No window pane
Looking out
And all I hear is possibility
All I see is possibility
My voice leaps and it's only afterwards that I see where I've landed
in hopscotch squares
Down the fire escape
Invisible footprints on the black marshmallow playground
Powerful and proud
Playfully prancing down St. Marks Street
Tickling the treetops with my toes
Laughter spilling into my most secret of secret gardens
My own unknown queendom
Where fresh melodies and pancakes melt with butter and real maple
syrup
In abundance
Where my friends and I time travel through black box theaters
Under rows of seating and large tables at artist gatherings
Playing hide and seek
My East Village element
My favorite concrete climate
Of make believe

A JOLT OF INSPIRATION

In 2012, after many years of studying Somatic Voicework™ and feeling very at home with my voice, I faced a new set of challenges with my physical health. After being able to joyfully eat anything I liked throughout my childhood, I started developing stomach troubles in high school, which then became more pronounced in my mid-30s. At that point, I began to experience food hangovers, heart palpitations, acid reflux, and overall lack of energy. I finally realized how bad it was when my husband and I rushed to the hospital, following a night of chills and uncontrollable shaking, in order to get an EKG.

The doctor declared that "everything was fine," but acknowledged the visible unsteadiness of my hands. She asked me if I had considered whether I might have anxiety, to which I answered, "I don't know... maybe. I'll do anything to stop this from continuing!" So, out of desperation, I decided to start working on a months-long program with a nutritionist recommended to us by our cousin, Lisa. It was a gradual, humbling, and often depressing learning process, but by that summer, I had come to accept my new dietary fate. I was on the mend, but nowhere near fully recovered, and I knew I needed something else to rejuvenate me.

That year, in July, I decided to travel to take a weeklong workshop in the countryside of Italy with singer/composer/educator, Anita Daulne. Anita is one of the founding members of Zap Mama—an Afro-Belgian a cappella group that launched in the 1990s and was all the rage. They toured all over the world, including at colleges like Oberlin (my alma mater), playing big music festivals such as SummerStage. They landed large, mainstream hits with collaborators, like Erykah Badu, and their cover of Phoebe Snow's "Poetry Man". Zap Mama refers to their music as "Afropean"—a mix of African and European music traditions, similar to the heritage of founding members, Anita Daulne and Marie Daulne. Marie still continues to drive the artistic vision of Zap Mama to this day.

Although the trip to Italy was challenging, it wasn't daunting because I knew something magical lay on the other side. Travel and music always have a way of curing my physical and emotional ailments. I had often been weak and dizzy for months. Things like sugar, alcohol, cheese, pasta, bread (what you might call the "sweetness of life") all exacerbated symptoms like feeling the room spinning or my hands itching with eczema. So, for the time being, I was on a rather strict diet—doing herbal cleanses (which were pretty exhausting) and eating lots of steamed vegetables, brown rice, nuts, fish, and chicken. I spent a great deal of my time focused on which foods I *could eat* without aggravating my symptoms and causing my energy to tank. In between the hours spent on my couch, I would teach a voice student or two, and then return to the waves of dizziness and minimal spark.

I learned that Anita was offering one of her weeklong intensives and, with my husband's encouragement, I booked a ticket to attend. Just the thought of it made me feel a bit better. As both a mom and a teacher, so much of my focus was spent inspiring and caring for others, but it was catching up with me. I needed a chance to be refilled. It was hard to leave Luna, our daughter—especially right in the middle of summer—but I also felt I wasn't being my best-mom-self, either. I thought that resting and learning, while giving my husband and daughter a week together, would hopefully do us all good. Plus, if I couldn't get what fuel I wanted from food, perhaps music could supply me with some vitality.

I arrived in Milan, Italy—first by plane, and then took a train to the countryside, and then secured a taxi into the hills. There, someone met me and brought me to a small chateau with a stunning view. I was delirious and a bit lightheaded from traveling while on a restricted diet, but I was grateful for the change and vast, beautiful landscape. I welcomed the opportunity to take a break from New York City, and I especially appreciated the change of pace in summer. On the day I arrived, I was able to unpack, explore, and settle in. Everyone participating in the workshop lived in the chateau, except for one woman—a German dancer who camped in a tent in the backyard—the rest of us shared rooms in the house.

Each morning, after taking turns washing up in the bathroom, we groggily made our way downstairs. French, Belgian, German, American—I was the only Black person there, apart from Anita and the Senegalese husband of the host. I was also the only American, which was refreshing, as conversations didn't always center around American culture. After breakfast—which usually consisted of coffee (which I didn't drink), bread (which I couldn't eat), fruit (which I could only eat in limited amounts), and eggs—we would start to activize with conversation and, inevitably, music.

Mealtimes were generally when people would start sharing snippets of songs and games they knew. Some of the attendees had taken workshops with Anita before, and some were also music teachers, and others were total music newbies. Altogether, there was quite a wealth of musical knowledge at the table, as well as curiosity. Once breakfast was complete, we would walk over to another nearby building on the property and begin learning whichever songs Anita had planned to teach us that day. After exploring songs from the Congo to South Africa, and spending hours learning parts, new rhythms, and harmonies, we would happily take lunch—our stomachs ready to refill what our brains had used up. Then, in the afternoon, we would resume learning more music.

I'll never forget that first day of singing. Without any preparation, long-winded intros, or warmup, Anita began to sing an up-tempo, two-step, polyrhythmic song, called "Bogi," about the story of a hot pepper. After several beats, everyone began to form a circle and tried their best to pick up the music. There was no discussion or big lecture, no time to think or analyze—only time to be oneself in the music. Move, sing, absorb.

It was pretty ironic—after weeks of sitting on my couch being hypervigilant about everything I did—there I was moving and digesting new information with very little difficulty. Still, it was a little nerve-wracking. Would my body punish me later? Would I become faint and need to hold onto someone to make it back home? I hated people seeing how feeble I actually felt, but I had been drinking herbal concoctions, monitoring my water intake, and keeping track of my energy output for so long that I didn't know what to expect. I just decided to say, "screw it!" It was healing, being less concerned with myself and others and just falling into the music.

We spent days like this—waking to the glorious sunshine on the hillside, doing yoga on the grass, filling ourselves with food and talk, and then singing songs chosen by Anita. She would pull them from her mental library and only share the written lyrics with us after we had lived with the material for a day or two. Every song had multiple sections, with multiple harmonies and rhythms to remember.

Sometimes, we broke into smaller groups to learn a musical phrase and movement. Sometimes, we would create movement ourselves. We sang everything a cappella, so we became the sonic beams and studs for the music. The interrelation of the group was the sole focus, there was almost no solo work, which was quite different from being a lead singer of a band. Sometimes, one section would lead, and then another, and as a result, Anita would emphasize that we had to play to the strengths of everyone in our group. If someone was having trouble learning a part or keeping a rhythm, then we needed to find a way to simplify it so that everyone could succeed and perform well.

Outside of learning music, there were a few trips to the gelateria. I may have allowed myself to sample a taste and swooned from the delights of refined sugar. When in Italy—pistachio, almond, coffee gelato—who can say no? We would usually walk to the center of town, some stopping to buy sweets as we slowly meandered along the cobblestone streets back to our house. At least once, we stopped at a plaza with a beautiful view, staying to sing for a while. For a moment, we became a wandering ensemble of modern troubadours, blissfully enjoying the liberation of our mobile instruments. Some days we would go to a near-by swimming hole. A few people would jog in the hot Italian sun while others walked. Once there, we would bathe in the water, fully clothed, and stretch out on various rocks afterwards to dry in the sun.

On the last evening, we prepared a final concert, which we then performed in a local square. After days of enjoying a rustic, yet beautiful setup, we were upgraded to lights, sound, and an audience. We each put on our nicest clothing for the event. I was surprised by the tingling nerves in my stomach and adrenaline racing through my body, temporarily replacing the tightness that usually inhabited my upper abdomen. I was nervous and excited. Since working with my nutritionist, I hadn't done much performing, and yet, miraculously, there I was—in another country, with people I hadn't known the week prior, singing and feeling alive.

It was a small gathering of children, parents, stray animals, and various characters from the neighborhood who had come out on a summer evening to witness this unusual group of singers. A local African dancer and drummers performed first, and then Anita gave our introduction. We sang a repertoire of Zap Mama songs—songs which Anita had learned from her travels throughout Africa, from her Congolese mother, and one Miriam Makeba cover. And then it was over. We celebrated with food and drink (much of which I couldn't have), and the next day, it was time to pack and head back home.

I had decided to stay in Milan before returning home. I'd found an apartment with a small, affordable room. It felt strange to be traveling alone again. I had grown accustomed to the many voices, anecdotes and storytelling of our week. We exchanged numbers and emails before parting ways, promising to stay in touch. But those connections would fizzle over time. Still, I was full.

Returning to the States, I felt slightly reborn—like I had been given a music transfusion. All the melodies from the retreat were playing over and over in my mind. For years, I could climb into the recesses of my mind and recall my time in Anita's "Afropean" workshop. It took a journey to the other side of the Atlantic to find my pulse again—to find that it wasn't only rice and beans—but sound which had resuscitated me.

A jolt of artistic inspiration had revitalized me. It was something no physician or nutritionist could have done. In the years to come, I went on to lead my own voice and movement workshops, and I would often teach at least one song I had learned from that trip. One of the songs, "Kombonayo," a song in Swahili, became a favorite of my daughter. The song's meaning translates to "peace"—a peace for which I am forever grateful.

ROLLER SKATES

If you want the magic elixir to life
    If you want to stay
        Forever Young
            Girl, put your roller skates on

                Freedom can be found, on the ground
                    Riding against traffic on 2nd Avenue
                  Freedom is the sound and glide
                      of tiny, plastic wheels talking over concrete
                                    not two,
                          but One
                    Roller Skate
                The power is in the step of your right
                and the push off of your left
            Slip one Roller Skate on
           Lace up
           Strings reaching for the skyyyyyyyyyy
      Make sure to bring a close Friend,
    Cousin,
Confidante
    Include collected change gathered from
        Dishes and piggy banks
           Spilled copper
                in between the planks
                    of your and her apartment floor
                      Forgotten pieces in pockets

And left in corners.

Put this together with your
Favorite sunglasses
and make your way to
any pizza parlor, Ms. Pac-Man and Prana,
Your favorite local health food store,

Supply yourself with all kind of super food for your
Spiritual transport - Magic carpet ride

Bring a sack for the two of you
to Capture
- Kasha knishes
- Dreams
- Boy crushes
- Wha Guru Chews full of
Cashews and Honey,
Malt and Almonds,
- Tingling sensations down your arms and between your legs
- Fresh apples
- And even apple cider

And then spin your wheel to fortune
Coasting down the boulevard
Riding against traffic on
2nd Avenue
6th Street
10th Street
Your intergalactic interlude
is unbound by traditional time travel
Though heavy at times
it will fit in a large backpack

or over the shoulder
Laces holding onto one another like close friends' arms
Freedom for those of us born in New York
New York to the bone and marrow
Freedom for those of us born in New York
was never in the shape of a car
It always slipped over your own two feet
or under your seat
or fit in your hand
Like a Graffiti can
or Microphone
Freedom for a New Yorker
Was something that spun from our minds
Like Cotton Candy
and rolled down the sidewalk
Leaving our stain
and memory
Like Ink
from The Village Voice
Young and Impressionable
Wise beyond our years
Collecting and repelling at the same time
like chewing gum

If you want the magic elixir to life
The secret sauce
With that special ingredient everyone is longing for
But rarely thinks to try
Strap on your Roller Skate Girl
Push off
and Rolllllllllllllll

Space to Create

VOICE LOG #13

I liked life. I liked imagining beyond what was.

ANOTHER 10 SQUARE FEET

"If you open up the window
And if you open up the door
You will see
Yes, you will see
Love and all its shining glory
Telling you a glory story
Telling you
And telling me...[1]*"*

—ABBEY LINCOLN

These are the lyrics from one of my favorite Abbey Lincoln albums, *People In Me*—an album that my mother played on our record player for much of my childhood. There are certain albums, like this one, that distinctly mark periods of my life growing up. I can still see the sturdy white shelf that sat in our front bedroom with the record player resting on it between the books and other objects. I can see Abbey's face, cast in blue light, on the album cover.

I remember other parts of our musical timeline in that apartment, as well. Joan Armatrading and Sting mark the years after my parents had separated and our apartment had been renovated. Stevie Wonder demarcates high school, and Prince specifically denotes my senior year

---

1 Lincoln, Abbey. "Living Room." *People in Me.* Inner City Records, 1978.

in high school. Lots of Prince! *King Pleasure* is probably one of the only records that helps me to see Chicago and the basement apartment my parents kept there before fully planting their feet in New York.

And Abbey? Abbey Lincoln overlaps the time when my parents were together and the time after, when they were separated. Maybe that's why her music, and this song in particular, resonates so much. There's a nostalgia and a hope at the same time. It's a sort of thread between worlds. Before their separation, our apartment had rough wooden plank floors that shocked you with splinters. Even though the splinters had been removed when our apartment was renovated, there was still something missing.

As much as I daydreamed about growing up, I didn't dream of big weddings, sweet-sixteens, or proms. The thing that I did fantasize about was space. I grew up in a one bedroom apartment, which my mom had arranged with the expert skill of a Martha Stewart type, yet I still envisioned the freedom that space could provide. The space that travel brings. Despite her low income, my mom did give me the experience of traveling. I went to a predominantly white school with mostly middle to upper-class kids, yet I had traveled to more places than most of them.

My mom and I journeyed to Italy, Israel, Brazil, France, Holland, Canada ("O Canada"), Mexico, and beyond. I have bathed in the Dead Sea, have eaten freshly baked croissants with butter and jam, have tasted newly-pressed olive oil, and have seen the celebrated Afro-Brazilian drumming group, Olodum, live in rehearsal—all because of dance. Dance had given my mom space, and therefore, gave both of us living room. Music, on the other hand, gave me my own space.

Staring out a window on a moving train or boat through Spain, listening to Jimmy Cliff's "The Harder They Come," as the landscape of Formentera stretched out before us. It created new storylines. Copious light and high ceilings, alternatively, could write new beginnings. The latter is what I imagine when I hear this song by Abbey Lincoln. The pleasure of open spaces and free time. It makes me think of all the couples—all the people—in the world, and what another ten square feet could give them.

Never in my wildest dreams did I imagine I would end up living in a house with a backyard. I never thought there could be any sounds outside my window other than honking horns and the traffic of voices calling out in the middle of the night. The only sounds I hear now are the slow, dragging inhales of my husband beside me, and the birds outside in our yard. Their rhythmic tweeting tells me they are much more awake than I am in the mornings, but I suppose even this, right now, could count as living room. All I hear are the birds, satisfied sleep, and the comfort of my own thoughts.

A REMEDY FOR ALL THINGS

A song will help most anything
A broken heart
A lost soul
A confused mind
Help soothe tears
Help soothe a cough
Help you to remember
And find what you forgot
A song will help most anything
I've heard
And that's what I know
Help when it rains and you're already late
Help when it snows
Help you in traffic
or when you stubbed a toe
Wanna scream so hard
Like biting your lip,
wanna break the damn window

A song will help most anything
Writer's block
Fishing for motivation
Deadlines' complication
Monday Blues
Winter Blues
Help you when your favorite team wins or lose

I've heard
And that's what I know

Help you to lift that 85-pound weight
Help pump you up before your blind date
To peel open your eyes when you still ain't really awake
A song will help most anything
I've heard
And that's what I know
Help you when you're feeling old
When there's too much ache and not enough pleasure in your bones
When you measure your height but wish you had more to grow
Help when it rains and you've gotta work late
Help when it's snows
A song can help most anything
Help you in traffic
Help children fall asleep when they're getting erratic
Eat every last bite
Before parents go into a panic
Help you when you look in the mirror
And don't like what you see
Help when your reflection is better than you expected it to be
Aye!
A song can help most anything
I've heard
And that's what I know
Help with standing in line
At the airport, post office, grocery "10 things and under sign"
A song will help you get the job done
Work all day long in the morning sun

When the alarm sounds and you're past ready for a break
Vision blurry from rereading that same sentence

Need help lifting that 85-pound weight
Carrying that load uphill
A song will help you write a song
Better than taking a pill
A song will help most anything
Help you find peace in the storm to be mentally still
Help when your loved one is gone
Help when you know it was them they meant to kill
A moan and a ramble will help you go on

A song will help move the movement
Help people to march
When your feet are tired
And your sole is losing its arch
Help keep the romance
When it seems the spark is low
Cause life gets harder than we know

A song will help quiet your fears
When they keep hanging around
A song will open your ears
To the music of life abound

A song will help learn your times tables
Or history dates
A song will help most anything
Give or take
But it's the give that a song will do
For anyone listening to
What's playing in the background/foreground for
Me, him, them or you
A song can help most anything
Wanting to be helped

A song can make you feel heard
And relieve whatever occurred
A song is often more significant than a word
A song will leave you forever stirred.

(HUMMING)

Oooooo
What a little humming will do
Ooooooo
What a little humming can do for you
Wait a while
Stay a while
Hum and let yourself dream a while
Oooooo
What a little humming will do

IT WILL REMAIN, LOVE'S REFRAIN

A cup
Half full
The garden wall
Nightingale
Roses bloom
It will remain paradise

-LOVE'S REFRAIN, 12/26/1996

When I was in college, my father remarried for the third and final time. I was in my first year at Oberlin when my father let me know that he was engaged to be married in the upcoming summer. I can still picture myself in my half of a tiny dorm room shared with my roommate, Logan. I was quietly stunned when I got the news—as one is when faced with a mix of competing feelings that they don't know how to process. I'm not sure who I told or how I told it.

Logan and I were still getting to know each other, yet we shared many intimate details of our lives with one another. This news was certainly not the usual college gossip or typical complaint. It was a combination of surprise, confusion, hurt, and joy all mixed up into one. I had no idea my dad had a love interest, and certainly had never met this woman who would become my stepmother, but he seemed happy and intent on tying the knot. Little did I know that this relationship would soon greatly affect my life.

My mother had also remarried a few years earlier, when I was in still in high school. I hadn't had much warning from her either. It felt like I met her boyfriend and, before I knew it, we were moving to California. Unfortunately, I never felt the same ease and connection with my stepfather as I eventually did with my stepmother. I'm certain this was difficult for my mom, and it also made it difficult for me to fully accept their marriage.

My dad's wedding took place in India. I was later sent photos of him with his mystery woman, smiling with the haze of newlyweds under frosted filters. Even though my father was much older than his wife, he, too, looked young. (Love changes people's faces, their texture, movements, and laugh.) I couldn't help but feel a pang in my heart—hurt acquired at not being invited to the wedding ceremony. (Decades later, this family split would repeat itself when I married my husband while my father was again away in India.) My father and his new wife relocated to New York shortly thereafter, and then I had the chance to meet her.

Senti, my father's wife, was a young Indian woman—noticeably younger than my father. Although she was officially my stepmother, it took many years for her to feel comfortable being called such. Her age made her feel more like a slightly older friend. However, being both a woman and closer to my own generation made Senti easier for me to get along with. Senti was quite short (around 5'2") with curvy legs, straight black hair, and a face that opened when she smiled. Although she was from India, she came from a place lesser known by most Americans in the northeast called Nagaland—a state further east than Nepal, Bhutan, or Bangladesh—where the appearance of the people tends to favor their neighbors to the east in Myanmar or Burma, rather than other parts of India.

Senti's family came from the mountains where the air was cool—not like the hot, sweltering days that one imagines when thinking of India. She and my father met when he was there on tour, and she was busy hanging out at her friends' music studios, recording commercial jingles, and bar-hopping at hotels in Mumbai. She was enjoying city life in her 20s when she and my dad fell in love. He said they should get married, and she agreed.

It wasn't long after my dad's wedding that my stepmother became pregnant with my younger sister—another surprise, at least for me. I already had one older brother from my father's first marriage, but since we grew up in different cities, we didn't see each other very often, and sadly, we aren't very close. The news of a baby sister felt like there was potential to build a closer relationship with a sibling. It was fun to imagine not being an only child—having someone to confide in, give advice to, and share inside jokes.

Little did I know that my desire to feel more connected and included in my father's life would be somewhat answered when, during my junior year of college, I got the chance to travel to India to see the new home he had bought. It was then I was introduced to the life he and my stepmother were making there. Goa had been one of the places they often visited during their courtship, so naturally, it inspired them to buy a house there. In Goa, I would meet my baby sister for the first time. Senti and my dad presented her to me swaddled on my pillow like a half-opened gift.

At just one month old, she was a perfect bundle. Nhumengula Threadgill, my father had named her. Just as my brother, Melin, and I had received made-up names, Nhumi (as we came to call her) inherited the most elaborate one. Nhumi was golden brown with reddish cheeks, straight black hair, sweet, and intensely focused on eating and sleeping. She was also like all babies—delicious, cuddly, and full of love, without trying.

I traveled to India with one of my oldest friends, Kate. Kate and I met at Friends Seminary in Mrs. Pillsbury's 8/9s class. At the time we met, she was huddled with a group of girls, whispering in one corner while I was goofing around in another corner. Somewhere between her Dr. Doolittle tendencies and her feverish need for change, and my daydreaming and feverish need to sing and dance—and both our needs to laugh endlessly about poop—we found a lasting friendship. Although our lives and families were very different, we weaved through one another's homes like sister vines—sometimes climbing beside one another, sometimes joined, sometimes spreading out and moving away, only to eventually end up beside one another again.

When my dad decided to bring me to India, he felt I should bring a friend. Since Kate and I had already traveled to so many places together—joining my mom on tour at Jacob's Pillow, or staying with her mom in Stone Ridge or Southampton, or journeying to places like Jamaica, where we indulged in Johnny Cakes and guava jelly, coffee with condensed milk, and jerk chicken—I naturally chose her as my companion. Going to India together felt like another chapter in the book of *Pyeng & Kate's Adventures*. India was a first for both of us, and we would be there for a long time.

It was the winter term which provided us with a full month off from school. Since we were traveling such a distance, we decided to settle in and really get to know the place. We both attended liberal arts colleges where the emphasis was as much on self-discovery as on world critique. Our plans for the month aligned quite well.

At Oberlin, winter term was a month in which you were required to do some sort of personal study of your own choosing. Students chose projects as varied as learning a new language, choreographing a dance, learning to ice skate, and studying Verdi. One year I studied midwifery, and another I researched my family tree. The year of our trip to India, I decided to write a book of poetry inspired by our travels. Kate was planning to paint. An avid painter at that point, she had already started building a significant portfolio. She rolled up several canvases and her oils, I packed my laptop and camera, and we were on our way.

Sweet juicy
salty dry
endless sky
unbroken field
cane crushed by teeth
sucked softly
Swallow the juice
Savor this
Little large supply

-12/28/1996

We began our trip with my dad, flying from New York to Mumbai. There was some sort of trouble with our luggage or tickets, and we kicked off the trip with my dad giving the ticket agents an earful—not an uncommon occurrence for him. With decades of touring as a professional musician—and as a Black man—he experienced countless airport agents, attendants, and people in general, second-guessing his intelligence and questioning how he made a living. These experiences left my dad with a very short fuse when it came to these types of mix-ups. After waiting in long lines and shuffling our way past countless bodies, we eventually got on the plane and began our 20-hour journey. The plane was packed with people and their necessities, comfort items, gifts, and all their individual idiosyncrasies.

We arrived in Mumbai late at night. We were hot and tired from all the traveling, as well as from the sudden change of climate. There were tons of people outside the airport, all with their own agendas. My dad—accustomed to the trip—got us a taxi to a hotel, where we stayed for the night, before returning to the airport the next morning to fly to Goa.

The flight to Goa was much smaller, with groups of young Israelis, ready to party, and Indian families heading off to vacation. By the time we landed in Goa, Kate and I were both spent. It took us a week to recover from the jetlag! I can't remember anything about our ride from the airport, except for the thrill I felt at seeing my dad's new home. I suddenly felt that the length of the trip had been worth the wait.

Having moved around between many different apartments in Clinton Hill, Brooklyn, my dad had never owned a home, and I had never known the pride and security of having a parent who owned a home. All my life I had grown up traveling with my wealthy, white friends to their country houses and unblemished apartments. For once, I could claim some part of that homeowner's legacy. And to see his home was truly like a taste of paradise.

At the same time, I knew this wasn't purely for me—it was for his new family. I was a close visitor with special benefits. Yet, it still gave me a sense of comfort—the kind of comfort felt in not having to tiptoe around a house or constantly ask before opening a drawer or cabinet. My dad's house was simple, yet glorious—especially to a couple of Bohemian college students.

It was situated on a small road in the mountains, far from the city center of Moira. To enter, there were several steps that led up to a tiled patio where one could sit and read, or stare at the horizon in the morning, or in the evening after siesta. There were large, wooden doors separating each room—perhaps a remnant of the Portuguese colonization of Goa. During the afternoons, we would close those doors and cover the windows to keep the heat at bay.

Inside there were plain, white walls and high ceilings. The first room you entered was a living room with low, minimal seating. Unlike the often overbearing and imposing leather couches of the Midwest, this furniture was adorned in beautiful, yet simple Indian fabric. To the left was my father's and Senti's bedroom, as well as a studio setup with a keyboard where my dad could compose music. To the right was Kate's and my bedroom, where we each received a pedicure to mark our arrival. There was a dining area in the center of the home, with the kitchen towards the back of the house and up a small flight of stairs. Behind the kitchen was a small room for Kate to use as a painting studio.

It took us a while to adapt to the time change, but soon enough, we began to find our rhythm. Each day was a celebration in eating. For each of us, including my baby sister, food was the center of everything. Kate and I would enjoy a light breakfast, consisting of some fresh fruit and cooked cereal, before going for a run in the neighborhood. The roads around my father's house were tiny, dirt roads that would then open into larger green fields such as rice paddies.

In the afternoons, after showering, Kate and I would enjoy a large lunch spread, artfully prepared by my parent's neighbor, Gulab, whom they had hired to cook and clean. There were always various curries and veggie dishes that we had never seen before like tendli and sana, a pancake bread made from coconut sap. Later, Kate and I would work on our own projects or venture into town.

Getting around Goa was a fun experience. As in many parts of the world, many people traveled by moped. My dad had a moped of his own for transportation, and Kate and I would take it to get around locally. This, in itself, was a comedy—the two of us peddling the ground like the Flintstones before taking off, laughing, and desperately trying to steer. Once we got the feel for it, it was a convenient way to get around town or to go to the beach.

We chose sunbathing over swimming in Goa, due to the over- whelming amount of jellyfish. On other days, my father would take us sightseeing, to markets, or to restaurants—one which was owned by the family of a college friend, Akash. While in Goa, I also decided to cut off my locs, which had grown past my shoulders and become a distinguish- ing part of my appearance. There was something about being in such an entirely new place with so much time to do with however I desired that made me crave a lighter head, both mentally and spiritually. I asked Kate to help me, and she nervously agreed, freeing each loc from its roots. When we finished, I buried my hair, along with old thoughts, in the ground outside my dad's home.

We lived well during our stay in Goa. Our days were like open pages ready to be filled with travel, movement, and art. Kate painted a series of blue, nude bodies, which I posed for; and I wrote poetry that chronicled my grandparents and my old loves, took pictures, and read. We exercised and enjoyed my dad's music collection. The soaring voices of Aretha Franklin's *Amazing Grace* album, Djavan, and La India carved the shape of those rooms, and our experiences, into our memories.

Each indigo figure Kate painted grew while my stepmother nursed my sister, who was also expanding with each passing day. My dad alternated between playing piano and being a new father and husband again. Our winter term had given us a new taste of life's possibilities. My head was several pounds lighter as I emptied ancestral stories onto the page. Our stomachs and hearts were full.

Grandaddy waz
Late nights
early mornings
chipped paint
Lover of Louis
Dedicated
and consistent
Brown as molasses
Blue like velvet
Graceful as chiffon
All day long

—"Like It Waz," January 1996

Your Sonic Voice

Hearing

Hearing Your Inner Voice

VOICE LOG #11

Right when I stopped thinking—I think I heard the real me.

ADJUSTING FOCUS

She's trying to hold steady, but really she's shaking inside. A slightly lightheaded feeling surrounds her, tho' no one can see all that it took to get here. Two trains and a Citibike—sweating to relax. Good thing she brought the extra smoothie from home. Taking risks takes energy, so she's gotta refuel. Under the lights, in front of the camera, inside the studio—she feels hot, humid, and goosebumps decorate her back and arms. It's not always easy being the first to make a sound. No one applauds your bravery.

Still, she places her legs in park to find her strength, and then it escapes. The ripples, hills, and canyons inside. No other map drawn quite like her. She hears her uneven borders. The narrowing of her dreams and the muting of her desires. She can feel walls of resistance, as her eyes glaze over, surrounding her like invisible soldiers. She doesn't know how to bring them down. Underneath layers and layers, a part of her hides, while another part shines.

She can hear her heart, it's not as loud as when she's performing. That pulsing, like miniature thunderstorms traveling underneath her skin, as she rhythmically transforms—filling with strength and ambition, then deflating with fear in the same measure.

Inside her throat lies the entire chronology of her life: Her parents, the hospital in Queens where she was born, the stars and constellations overhead at the time, her favorite color, favorite book, favorite singer, her best friends from elementary school, and the rifts between them after high school and college, the boy who stood too close, the girl who didn't stand close enough, her idiosyncrasies, her love of speed, her disdain for being rushed, her fear of seeing it all pass by too soon, of not making the right choices or not being able to serve her choices justly, her love of powerful voices, and fear of vulnerability. Just like this moment.

With only a month and a half left before the concert, her mind is a swirl of details—planning logistics, practice sessions, dream outfits, email addresses, and calendar dates. Sometimes, her vision gets cloudy from all the effort put into focusing. Always adjusting her focus. Maybe that's why her lens always seems to need cleaning. It isn't really *her* lens, but the way in which she is pointing the camera. Too often looking out, instead of in.

But in the studio, with her teacher, she is the exposed image. The thing that she normally tries to avoid behind music stands, solos, and other voices. An exaggerated enlargement of her hesitation and insecurity. Sometimes it doesn't feel so intense, but today it's particularly raw. And right now, amid rawness, she has to take the first step—again. Whether graceful or clumsy, she has to leap.

She's trying to hold steady, but really she's shaking inside. A slightly lightheaded feeling surrounds her skin, tho' no one can see all that it took to get here. Under the lights, in front of the camera, inside the studio—she feels hot, humid, and goosebumps decorate her back and arms. It's not always easy being the first to make a sound.

HIDDEN COMPASS

Your voice is thunder clapping
Lightning striking your world
Tiny ripples in a pond
Moving out like a raft of ducks

A rushing stream
Telling you which way to go
Which foot to put down where
Who to trust

Your voice is the undercurrent
A stream of beliefs, feelings, preferences
Rumbling below
Your wounds
Their time to heal
And your impatience

Your voice is a genius idea
An innovation
A worthy contribution

Who needs words to make a beautiful sound?

SEEING IN THE DARK, OR NIGHT VISION

You're looking for a figure, or something familiar—an outline, a landscape, a cushion, or some kind of warmth that is reminiscent of something you heard or touched. But it's nowhere to be found. Only cold corners, abrupt endings, ungraceful and unsatisfying forms. It can feel lonely, discouraging, and even humiliating trying to find your voice—especially in the dark.

No one tells you that you will be searching in low light. That you will very often find yourself alone. Comforted, yet disappointed; ecstatic, but terrified; yearning and inspired, but often alone. But it makes those moments of togetherness, with connective music-making-tissue, so sweet! So delicious! Like the new tastes and smells of far-off places. An unexpected, syrupy embrace. Fragrant, like mint and lavender, smooth like your freshly oiled hair, and infinite as ocean shores blending into the sky.

Experiencing togetherness while creating music will make your heart beat, and open, and beat again—in the same way that having a child throws you into new dimensions. In the same way that seeing a good friend after years transcends time. Everything in that moment will feel like enough.

Until you are back in your practice. Peering inside yourself in complete darkness. A new unknown. How do you know if this is good? Or right? Or better than the last time? Is *this* sense of better enough? It might sound worse. You might feel worse. And then you will need to remember to hang on.

Make sure to leave yourself some breadcrumbs, some sealed letter, or message in a bottle to read so that you can remember to *sing any-*

way. Because little do you know, but you are developing a new sight. A stamina for seeing in the dark. For feeling and finding without artificial light or approval. You are locating yourself without the same emotional landmarks as before, and each time you show up, you will find yourself more quickly, because you ventured alone, because you allowed it to be different, unexpected, and unknown.

JOURNEY AHEAD

When you're alone in your room

Singing with all the dedication of a devout yogi,
Next Pop sensation,
Monk or
John Coltrane,

You may grow bored,
You may grow lonely,
You may get discouraged.
You may start to see the journey ahead
And only sense   miles and miles and miles

In the distance.

With tears streaming down your window
and little visibility
You will probably wish that the walls could talk
That the heater would reassure you
That the carpet could console the tenderness of your pride
yet when they do,
You might want to take it back.

Tell them
Keep their thoughts to themselves.

So instead,

Close your eyes,
Soften your heart
Breathe in,
And sing out.

Fear of Being Heard

VOICE LOG #65

Is it really gonna be safe out there?...being seen

SURROUND SOUND

Do you ever hear the sound of your voice echoing in the air around
you and wonder
Why is it so shrill today?
Where is the body?
Who is that squeaking and whining,
croaking and frying,
rushing and gasping?

Do you ever hear the sound of your voice sounding in the air around
you and wonder
Who's this person?
So large,
Powerful,
Loud and fierce,
So unapologetic

And do you ever hear the sound of your voice in the air and wonder
How long will this take?
For me to become the me that I truly want to be.

SHAKY GROUND

You never know what you're going to get from the sound of a new voice—what you'll receive as a listener and what the singer will learn about themselves. Before students come to work with me—either in Alexander Technique, Somatic Voicework™, or a combination of the two—I always ask what it is that they are looking for and why. I don't only ask students to do this—I've also had to ask myself these same questions.

In order to be the best teacher I can be for my students, I have regularly pondered, "Who do I want to work with?" Do I want to teach professional singers or do I want to teach someone simply wanting to learn more about how to sing? I enjoy teaching people who want to learn about singing or improve their singing in a holistic way, beginner or professional. People who honor both technique and feeling—their personal lives, as well as professional lives. As it turns out, not everyone wants that, nor have they thought of it as an option, and not everyone teaches voice this way.

I once worked with a student named Nicole. A former dancer in her late 20s, Nicole was exuberant and highly motivated. She was at a point in her career and life where she had space to reflect and find new direction, so she decided to use the time to invest in one of my voice and movement programs. Two things that were great about Nicole were her commitment to practicing and her drive. She wanted to sing and perform, so she began taking practical steps and showing up to do the necessary work to make that happen.

Because of her desire to sing in public, coupled with her self-discipline, more and more opportunities became available to her over time. She and her boyfriend wrote music and performed together. Their circle of friends often called on them to write personalized love songs for weddings and other special occasions.

Initially, Nicole felt awkward when singing high notes, what voice teachers and singers refer to as head register. She didn't feel like it fit her personality. When Nicole was growing up, other girls in school with naturally high voices, often labeled sopranos, would get selected for lead roles and solos that stood out. Nicole didn't have a naturally high speaking and singing voice, so she didn't think she would ever be able to comfortably sing a soaring vocal part. But, as is the case with every new student, the first thing we worked on was developing and strengthening Nicole's head register.

In my monthly online vocal warmup, Vocal Gym, Nicole started to apply changes to her singing. I saw her committing to mouth shapes that would free her jaw and help stretch her vocal range. I saw her breathing intentionally in order to expand her vocal stamina. I watched Nicole learn to get out of her own way. In our private sessions, she allowed herself to vocalize much higher than any of her music dictated. At times, I would have to reassure her that it was alright if her voice cracked or seemed a bit flat or "thin." More than anything, I wanted her to get used to hearing her head voice without reacting by tightening her throat.

Months went by. Nicole and her partner were asked to sing at friends' weddings, at birthday parties, at spiritual ceremonies, and more. Nicole started to feel more confident. She was doing the thing that she said she wanted to do. She felt joyful and at ease being in front of people. Her experience as a dancer served her well in this way. At the same time, she would regularly question whether she was good enough, strong enough, or talented enough to be a "real" singer. She wondered whether she had sung on pitch or sounded strained.

I reminded her of how much progress she was making, as we gradually worked on building her higher register. It's easy to say you want to improve, but then not practice; or to practice compulsively, yet constantly criticize yourself. It takes finesse to practice consciously and recognize your growth while also acknowledging that you still have farther to go. I hoped to help Nicole with the latter.

Singing is a bit mysterious—you need to listen to your voice, while at the same time not listening to it. At times, I've observed—both in my teaching and in my own practice—that staying connected and listening to my body is of greater importance than listening to the sounds I'm making. As a trained dancer, I wanted to help Nicole to listen to her instincts and to channel her physical and emotional energy into singing. To breathe in, sing out, and discover what was there. To allow herself to make an unexpected sound and witness it. I know this is harder than it seems.

I've observed many students stop themselves from allowing this to happen for fear that they would make a mistake. The challenge is to practice regularly enough, and trust in the process, so that you start to believe in your ability to stick the landing. You must enter the process by being intentional, being aware of your body, sensing your breath before you sing, and while you sing, and allow your voice to surprise you.

At first, it might feel like you are hanging in the balance, fearfully wondering, "What is my voice going to do this time?"—and so many times you don't hit the note. Sometimes you almost hit the note, but miss. Other times you hit the note gracefully, but it's inconsistent. It isn't easy to detach yourself from your performance when you're so uncertain of your voice. But gradually, over time, Nicole, like so many others, was able to connect with her head register. Her perseverance in that unpredictable, shaky place started to garner results.

For most people, the shaky ground is right in their break, which is where the chest register, or speaking voice, and head register meet. Except, the thing is, the two parts of one's voice don't usually meet—it's more like an abrupt gear shift. For most people, one register in their voice is more dominant than the other, and as a result, people tend to feel exposed and out of control when they are in the non-dominant register. Although I explain this to students in their initial trial lessons, it still requires regular reminders. It takes a lot of stamina to remain vulnerable while practicing in that register. For most students, this is the source of many fears, embarrassment, and frustration.

Sometimes it's just plain old frustrating when your voice won't do what you tell it to do. Other times a singer may desire to be seen, but there is also a conflicting desire to hide, to stay small and quiet. Maybe someone once told them they didn't have a good voice, or laughed at them, or told them they were too loud. Maybe they had parents who told them to stop crying, to hold in their feelings, or that children are meant to be seen and not heard, or maybe they messed up in a school concert once and they have never been able to live it down. (I had a student at NYU once admit that the reason they had signed up for the class I was teaching was because he had had a humiliating singing experience in the past, and never wanted to live through such a thing again.)

Flopping in a performance can feel like one of the worst visceral experiences in the world! (Like that infamous dream people have where they are standing naked at the front of a classroom.) For this reason, I encourage and urge people to make new and unfamiliar sounds in order to grow accustomed to the unexpected but also to build an archive of dependable, familiar sounds. I say this as someone who has been performing on stage since I was 3 years old. I realize that for many people, who have no intention to perform, that simply speaking to another person, or in front of a group, can feel terrifying. To sing is an act of revealing. What would motivate you to go to a dangerous place, a place that feels as dangerous as the earth moving underneath your feet?

In order to get stronger, sometimes you have to take a step back and allow everything to quake a little, to be unsteady. Within the uncertainty of that shaky space is where most of us can connect with one another on an emotional level. Although we don't think of singers like Etta James as having "thin" sounding voices, when she sings a lyric like, "I would rather go blind;[2]" or when Stevie Wonder says, "I never dreamed you'd leave in summer[3]"—we feel the fragility of that person intertwine with our own fragility.

---

2   Etta James. "I'd Rather Go Blind." *Tell Mama.* Cadet, 1968.
3   Stevie Wonder. "Never Dreamed You'd Leave in Summer." *Where I'm Coming From.* Tamla, 1971.

We feel the vulnerability of being human—hurt, lost, failing, shamed, rejected, and wanting to hide, but instead, daring to sing out. There's something about singing out, despite our pain and inadequacies, that connects us to other humans every time. It's not a surprise that songwriters and composers often write about this, but it also shouldn't be a surprise that training your voice requires you to cover the same ground. At this point in my practice, I know that even when I am singing on shaky ground, I've sung there many times before, and I know that my voice has strength in the seemingly delicate, or attenuated, parts. Of course, I know I'll never be a Patti LaBelle belter, but every voice has its own power. As for Nicole, she began to discover the thrill of singing lay in allowing her voice to be a space for her truths and the truths of others to both be seen and heard.

RESISTANCE

It grows   and grows
Like a plant
Like the sun
Getting hot and hotter
Large and larger
Stabs in my abdomen
      Twinges
            Shocks
                It grows

Every time my body grows weak
My mind grows smarter
Smelling, licking, tasting
Sharpening my knife to cut out a place for me
To cut out words and melodies
To evict the vines wrapping around my legs and throat

To cut out these pages of make believe
Where white, foreign men attempt to trample
The soft, wild parts of me

Sneaking up on me in the dark
Blurring my vision
No matter how many times
I tell my body "relax"
Remind myself "it's safe here…

...No one's out to get you"

Only that's half true

Resistance seeping into my bloodstream
Into my veins
Like a slow-motion dance
Between opposing liquids
Vinegar and oil
My mother's shadows
My father's ghosts
Floating in my unconscious
Until I pull them out of the water to dry in the sun
Getting hot and hotter
Like winded children
They ask to be held

Why resist a good thing?
My mind smelling, licking, tasting
Sharpening my knife to cut out a place for me
To cut out words and melodies
Crouched underground
Sweating in a jail cell
Bleeding on the operating table
Shot at the podium
No one's out to get you
No one's out to get you
No one's out to get you

FITTING INTO THE MOLD

I wonder how far back in time we would have to go to arrive at the point when humans first became fearful about making and sharing art. What event happened at that particular moment? Did someone suddenly have to dance to save their child's life or sing for days on end or else their tribe would starve? It makes sense that any rite of passage would bring with it some level of anxiety or worry, but art seems different. Has it always been human nature to feel some sort of imposter syndrome, performance anxiety, or pressure to be the best? Or did this arrive with colonialism, classism, patriarchy, and the push away from indigenous ways of being? Since art hasn't always functioned the same way in society, it seems hard to believe that our role as artists, as well as our interpretation of that role, hasn't changed with it.

Over time, painting, sculpture, music, dance, and theater have gone from a spiritual balm, a political mobilizer, a means to mourn, integrate and celebrate, to a commodity—a quick exchange, easily consumed as fast as take-out from In-N-Out Burger. This speed of consumption often disrupts the potential for art to foster deeper insights, group connections, self-discovery, and overall healing. Instead, community-building contests have evolved into large corporate industries such as *American Idol* and *Dancing With The Stars* where streaming networks ooze a strange circus of competition and celebrity worship. These ways of thinking embed themselves into many people's psyches as feelings of inferiority, rather than empowerment.

I spend a lot of time thinking about art and fear, how it manifests, why, and what to do with it. How "perfect" should I be? How and when, as a teacher and a performer, should I just say "fuck it, it's good enough," and embrace the art-making moment? And when do I continue mining for a shinier, or perhaps, more "coherent" final piece? As a voice and movement teacher/mentor, I walk a fine line between wanting students to refine their work, and wanting them to commit to a consistent practice that both supports and challenges them—that nourishes them and takes them someplace new, where authentic expression blooms.

However, I also recognize that we live in interlocking systems of oppression that greatly impact our mindsets. Systems that tell children that they are not enough as they are. They are not enough because they are Black, because they are gay, because they are female, because they are trans, because they are short, because they do not speak English, because they are fat, because they are poor, because they are biracial, because they are rich, because they are not American. For any reason, at any time of day, especially in America, one can be caught questioning themselves and their self-worth. As Americans, with a historically dominant Christian influence, we are often taught that this can then be remedied by working to improve oneself, usually by buying some product and/or repenting. I go through a tug of war both between my own philosophy and practice regarding how much editing and fine-tuning I should do in my performance and how much self-love and acceptance I need.

Rather than actually honing in on musical parts while I'm rehearsing with other musicians, I tend to like to play a song over and over, until the playing of the song and its players creates an ideal arrangement organically, through repetition. Although I don't practice a specific religion, I would liken this to the function of trance-like states within various spiritual contexts. Some might argue that the way in which I fail to write things down and definitively set all parts is lazy. I can imagine many professors, professional players, and students finding this to be a subpar approach. But on the contrary, when I arrive at the time for rehearsing with other collaborators, I'm listening for when my body responds positively to a gel, or syncing, in the music. I believe that this comes from the intentions of the musicians working together, but it also comes from how I am connecting to myself at the moment.

My preference for collaborative music arranging began as early as middle school and continues to the present. However, at 25, I experienced an event which placed fear and music closer than they had ever been before in my life. I had the good fortune of getting a record deal and also the blessing of becoming pregnant at once. Soon into the process of rehearsing for my album *Sweet Home: The Music of Robert Johnson*, I discovered I was eating for two, and I became concerned how one gestation would fit with another. So rather than gloating about my pregnancy, I hid it. My husband knew, our parents, and a few close friends knew, but no one in my band or studio was aware. I would line my bag with pretzels and other snacks to keep from getting sick while listening to playbacks. Watching the meters for distortion, I monitored my own uncontrollable expansion—trying not to do anything out of the ordinary.

With a growing baby inside my belly, I was worried about how motherhood would play into my vision of myself as a touring musician, recording vocalist, and bandleader. How "perfect" should I be? How put together should I appear? In essence, I wondered how close to a man's experience was I supposed to have? I was nauseous, I was scared, I was nauseous because I was scared. A part of me also felt slightly detached from what was happening—like I wasn't fully in my body, but instead, I was watching my life play out on a TV screen, wondering who that person was. I didn't recognize her.

Since my friends were, like me, in their mid to early 20s, most of them weren't married, or pregnant, or full-time artists. So I couldn't find the sisterhood I was longing for. I desperately needed someone sitting in all three experiences as I was, especially another Black woman. My mother told me early in my pregnancy, encouragingly, that I would be able to do whatever I wanted as an artist and mother. Even though I didn't fully believe her, I tried to ignore the doubting voices in my head. The truth was apparent in the music scene at large. In the coming years when I looked at other artists who were successfully headlining jazz festivals and clubs like those in which I was performing, I saw mostly single, childless women.

My musician friends joke that my husband and I were pioneers–
that we gave them the courage to forge ahead in building families of
their own. But while I was going through it, I didn't feel like a pioneer at
all. I felt like most people standing up to sing for the first time in front
of a group of people—exposed and scared. I see the many silver linings
now. As a result of my trips and falls, I've built a practice that reflects all
parts of me. I'm no longer trying to fit into someone else's vision of who
I should be. And I've learned that, although it's a slower process, there's
power in making art while honoring my family, my personal life, as well
as my creative vision. Hopefully, this is what future artmaking continues to look like—a process where art and art-maker override hundreds
of years of oppression—where technique and rigor are considered as
much, if not more, than connection and liberation.

DANCING WITH THE DEVIL
(f minor)

Dancing with the devil
I'm doing a slow grind
Dancing with the devil
Feels like I'm losing my mind

Oh I'm waist deep
In the mud
I'm half asleep
Just because

Oh I'm blind
Don't want to see
A wrinkle in time
Holding me
It feels good
It feels good

Dancing with the devil
I'm doing a slow grind
Dancing with the devil
Feels like I'm losing my mind

Oh how I'm full
But still hungry
Taking crumbs
For my safety

He grabbed my leg
With lock and key
Why didn't I wait
Patiently?
It feels…

And when my well is dry
He blocks the sun
He holds my hand
And dries my eye
(Takes a stand
On wet land)

Oh I'm waist deep
In the mud
I'm half asleep
Just because

Oh I'm blind
Don't want to see
A wrinkle in time
Holding me
It feels good
It feels good

Dancing with the devil
I can't keep up
Dancing with the devil
He keeps filling my cup

Dancing with the Devil
He quenched my thirst
Dancing with the Devil
His needs always first

Dancing with the Devil
Dancing with the Devil
Dancing with the Devil

BITTER/TRUTH

Cold
Midwest, Minnesota cold
Sneaking inside your collar
Climbing your spine
Waking you without asking
A torso in contraction
Sour lemons and lime
Teeth chattering
Sometimes it's a grind
And bitter
Bitter like winter

Fragile
Like broken pieces glued together more than once
Healing wounds
And itching scars
Scaly
Desperate to Hide
Sometimes it's fragile
And tender headed
Like thick haired girls
And bitter
Like dark greens

Shame
Nervous sweat
Strong smell(ing)
Hot too fast
uNcomfortable
Uncontrollable bowels
Hidden under obedient clothing
Goosebumps, dampness
Shaking and waking with a start
Sometimes it's bitter
Like truth

UNSOLVED MYSTERIES

P.S. 15 Elementary School, New York City, 1:15pm

A classroom of 3rd graders sits in rows at their desks to start a new Math lesson. Backpacks rest on the floor, various hoodies and tshirts hang over the backs of their seats. At the front of the class the students happily watch a new problem forming on the chalkboard. In the second to last row a young, Black girl sits frozen in her seat.

ANY YOUNG GIRL

I don't like it. I don't like it! I don't want to be here. No, I don't want a turn. I'm not good at this, anyway. How come she keeps looking at me? I don't know the answer.

Mrs. Crigler keeps saying try, and then makes that face when someone gets it wrong. I don't want to tell anybody anything. Nope! I'm not raisin' my hand.

I need the *right* answer.

I want a *good* idea! I want a good idea! One that's sparkly and shiny, and one that makes the *whole* room look—one that makes everyone look *twice*. Like, "Ooooo! How did she know that?" But I don't have anything. Nothing special. It's just plain, old me. I don't have anything in my lunchbox. Nothing in my pockets.

My house is just brown, broken floors.

ANY YOUNG GIRL sighs slumping into her chair

No shiny countertops, no new clothes. My kitchen has a bathtub in it, and a window near the stove where the pigeons poop outside.

My house doesn't sparkle and shine. Sometimes there's a homeless person sleeping on the floor when we come home late at night, and sometimes our neighbor's boyfriend is mean to her, and last year someone stole my Snoopy doll at McDonald's. Even though my mom asked, and looked and looked, no one found it.

ANY YOUNG GIRL perks up

I like my things, but I don't want anyone else to see. I don't have the kind of clothes like the kids at school have. I have a loft bed, close to the sky, where I can hide away and think allllll kinds of things my parents don't know about, 'cause they can't see.

When it's cold in the morning, I watch tv and get dressed under the covers. There's no doorman in our building, or washing machine. We don't live in a building with lots and lots of apartments where you can ride the elevator, and trick or treat on every floor, and make up mysteries. We don't even have an elevator, just stairs. Big, black, stone stairs.

But I could solve A LOT of mysteries.

I could be a detective one day. I'm *always* solving mysteries around the house and at rehearsals, at my mom and dad's jobs, and no one even knows it. Grown-ups are always leaving clues around, thinking that no one else can see them. One day I'm gonna have big ideas and solve *big* mysteries and everyone will come from all over to hear how many words I can say in Spanish and to see me dance…'cause I'm gonna be a ballet dancer, too. Mmm hmm….and then I'll go to my police job in between. Yep, there'll be time. I'm gonna be a policewoman, just like my Aunt Tina. She's bossy and fast and has long legs, like me. I could be a good police officer. I like to tell people what to do. *The same way grown-ups do*—like my dad and my Aunt Tina and Grandma Rose. Grandma Rose is always telling me to "be quiet" when I'm walking down the stairs…but I *am being quiet!*

Not quiet like right now tho'…right now I'm being really really quiet. 'Cause I don't want anyone to see. I don't want anyone to see me right now, my hair or my house. I don't want anyone to hear me right now 'cause I don't know the answer to Mrs.Crigler's question!

But when I'm walking down the stairs at Grandma's house, I like to sing all my favorite songs. I CAN SING LOUUUUDDDD! I like getting called on to sing in music class.

I like yelling…just 'cause…and singing and dancing and laughing and laughing…and talking…and

I like ChapStick—the kind that tastes sweet when you lick your lips. I like to eat that kind.

My mom likes to talk *a lot,* too, and dance and sing songs really loud… until she doesn't, and then she's very quiet. Blegh! So quiet that the whole house gets quiet. The table and chairs and all the plants. No, thank you! I don't like being around her when she's *that* quiet. I want to go outside and play with somebody. I don't like *those* kinds of mysteries.

I don't go inside other people's diaries. That's not right. People should be allowed to have some secrets they keep to themselves. Some secrets they can share if they want. But my mom, her secrets are behind her eyes, like two big ponds swishing around our house. I *really* don't want to hear about all her mysteries.

I'd rather go outside and meet my friend, Fantasia. We can count how much money we have and then go ride our roller skates and get pizza and play video games…like Donkey Kong. I LOVE Donkey Kong! And after we could make waffles at her house, or mine's, because we both have waffle makers and we both have real maple syrup. I have butter! But she has vegan margarine.

That's still good.

Sometimes when we go to her house her mom is reaaaalll quiet too. Just sittin' and staring at the tv. How come moms always look sad?

    ANY YOUNG GIRL pauses as if waiting for an answer from the audience

They should have a place for sad moms to be together where kids don't have to go. A place where moms can go and make each other feel better 'cause they have the same kind of secrets.

It's fine with me, so long as I don't have to be around my mom being sad, and then angry. Like, she's just angry at everything. Angry at this and angry at that, and I should clean up or do the laundry or blah blah blah blah blah. But doesn't she know it's not fun being around her when she's like that?! Why can't there be *any* other kids or fun grown-ups to come over? I don't want to be here! I don't.

    ANY YOUNG GIRL notices her teacher watching.

And why is Mrs. Crigler *still* looking at me? I don't know the answer. I'm just good at solving some mysteries, not all of them.

Blackout.

Nourishment

VOICE LOG #32

All these people came to help, more than I realized.

CREATING BOUNTY

In the East Village, we were used to walk-up apartments—steep stone steps and narrow hallways to lead you to your sanctuary. No elevators or doormen who knew all the names of your family members and pets to greet you. Outdoor space was the fire escape, and "appliances" were your trusty toaster or the oven broiler.

We ate out of refrigerators that were half the height and width of a traditional one, in order to fit into uniquely small or awkward spaces. Instead of loading a dishwasher, you washed the dishes and dried them by hand or sat them on a rack to dry. This is still the case for many New Yorkers, but not for my daughter and her friends—for them it's mostly history like the telephone and typewriter. All these seemingly random parts of our environment were key signs of my parents' decision to build creative lives.

My mom didn't shop at big box stores or eat at chain restaurants— she and I shopped for our groceries every day or so. We bought fresh vegetables from the neighborhood Korean markets, fresh pasta from the cheese shop, sweetened pies, and pancakes with honey and real maple syrup. Eating nutritious food was regularly emphasized in my household. My mom bought rye, sourdough, and multigrain breads before artisanal was a trend—breads with sturdy crusts, embedded with walnuts and caraway seeds from the health food store. There was no Costco or Trader Joe's. No private shopper to wheel your groceries home. We had to lug them up the stairs ourselves and make it all fit in a few small kitchen cabinets. Everything had to have a place because space was limited.

Sometimes my mom bought enough food to last us several days, or she would buy meals from the Polish diner, Teresa's, or the Chinese food place around the corner. While many of the kids at my school had steady cleaning ladies and babysitters, I thought it was strange that I ate better than most of them. Later I would come to understand that wealth isn't solely tied to money, and that being nourished could happen through food, as well as community, which explains why I never felt poor.

We had wealth, but not in the form of expensive material things. We didn't have anywhere near the financial cushion that most of the kids at my school had. If ours was a cushion, it was a worn-down sliver of foam, too hard for sitting. Despite rehearsing and touring, working various jobs in waitressing and construction, and being without the support of a steady partner, my mom built our wealth through friends, adventure and delicious, nourishing home-cooked meals, served regularly in a tidy home.

Seasoned black beans, brown rice with steamed broccoli, vegetable quiche with sunflower seed toppings. My mom became so fixated on quiche for a period that I had to officially boycott it, although I would later discover the utility of quiche, once I had my own child. She made string beans with garlic and fresh ginger, tortellini pasta with fresh olive paste, cooked sardines with caramelized onions, served with a large salad—so good that anyone anti-sardine would be converted. She made our meals with fresh, affordable ingredients—meals made with love— love for me, but also for life itself.

After my parents separated, my mom entered a new phase in her dance career and began working with the up-and-coming Urban Bush Women. When she joined the company, I doubt she realized she would be touring and teaching nearly half of the year. The Urban Bush Women quickly evolved into a new, groundbreaking dance theater company led by choreographer Jawolle Willa Jo Zollar. The company was an all-Black, female group of dancers, singers, and actresses with a vision to tell Black American/underrepresented stories and connect with communities through dance. When they first began performing and having success, Jawolle noticed that most of the audiences they performed for were white. The Black people were often behind the scenes—working in service as janitors, cleaning staff, and secretaries—instead of in the audience. So, she started looking for ways to share her work that would draw Black audiences, and this is what transformed her company into more than just a dance company. Through their commitment to teaching the arts, dancing, and storytelling, they also became known for community engagement and activism.

At first, the Urban Bush Women mostly worked throughout New York, but their success grew quickly, and my mom, like my father, became a busy, touring artist. This meant she had to juggle caring for me, working other jobs in between dancing, maintaining her training as a professional dancer, and tending to her own personal needs. So, what does a single mother do when she has to go on tour? She brought me with her! My mother took me with her to Sao Paulo, Bahia, New Orleans, Amsterdam, San Francisco, you name it. And I wasn't just brought along—I was made a part of the cast. I was a stand-in for other dancers, a singer, babysitter, and anything else that Jawolle and the rest of the company thought of.

When I wasn't on tour with my mom, I would stay with close friends, like my friend Kate and her mom, Linda, or one of my mother's friends, like Sophie Pujebet. Yet another example of someone hedging their bets on the arts, Sophie was a French jeweler who lived in a 5-story walk-up on East 2nd street, and owned a beautiful jewelry boutique in the East Village. Living with Sophie meant entering a tropical universe—the residents of her building had painted their hallways, transforming their building's interior into a lush jungle.

Sophie's apartment was one of the only other apartments I knew of that still had a bathtub in the kitchen, just as our apartment originally had, before being renovated. Her building was primarily inhabited by artists. Together, the tenants put out their own building newsletters showcasing their opinions on art, politics, and more. They painted their black, tar rooftop to look like a wild garden landscape. For one to two weeks, I would move in with friends like her or Kate, or my friend Anya. They fed me and made sure I was taken care of while my mom was away carving dances on stages across the country. Singing songs about love and lipstick, housing and determination, she was providing for the two of us.

Looking back, I know some part of me would have preferred we both stayed home. The love I received was affirming, but the constant moving from home to home was not. I wanted to stay close to our tiny kitchen and it's half-size fridge, our plates full of egg foo young and the reassurance that the next day would be a repeat of our shopping ritual at the corner market. I wanted my ride home on the M14 bus, the dates to KFC with Cavana that culminated in us belting out Whitney Houston's "Saving All My Love For You."[4] I wanted that shared experience of witnessing our moms pursue their dreams. And I wanted days that ended with a visit to Sophie's for dinner; to look out on the bounty of her building's tar painted flower garden as we watched the sunset.

---

4   Whitney Houston. "Saving All My Love For You." *Whitney Houston.* *Arista,* 1985.

DAWN

Confiding into her pillow
Blues and greens
Pink lists of dreams
She wakes soft, then loud
Her voice is like an aroma
Wild and earthy,
Singing along to the radio
Dancing on the cracks of her kitchen floor
Humming a tune
No one thought of
She invokes incantations in the shower
Amongst salt and eucalyptus
To cut the clinging grease of life
Conversing with herself
Between stretch marks and soft flesh
She shares fear and resentment with her epidermis
Waiting for it to cringe
and recoil
But the thoughts only slide off and melt down the drain
In a concoction of soap, skin and hair

She's groggy and restless
But recommits to the promises she's made herself
Her voice
Slides out like smoke and flames

Wafting upwards
Like everyone
She cried herself into existence
and still the sound of her laugh
Remains unapologetic
Holding onto
Melodies and memories
Letting them Re-member her
and the minerals that forged her constitution
Those which give her potency
and Power
She used to question
Their reason
Now she just savors their rhyme

FORMENTERA

For years now I've been wanting to write a song entitled "Formentera." I started the song several years ago, but the sound didn't match my memory of the experience. I thought writing about it might allow me to better convey the memorable adventure that my mom and I took to that tiny Balearic island off the coast of Spain decades ago.

When on tour with my mom, I often would end up standing in for one of the dancers. During tech rehearsal, when someone had to get a prop, run to the restroom, or perhaps rehearse a particular section of choreography on the side—I would then find myself singing, spinning, dancing, enacting deaths, having fits of laughter, or in states of spiritual rapture in order to help the lighting and sound crews gather their cues. For one tour, we had gone to Montpellier, France, and I wasn't just a stand-in—this time I had my own role in the performance, *Shelter*.[5]

Shelter was an evening-length collaborative work about the epidemic of homelessness. Full of pride at having an official role, I walked from position to position, shifted in space, and sang, "Shelter, looking for some shelter." Little Asmahan, the daughter of Robin Wilson, another company member, and I wandered the stage together, in search of a home, as the rest of the dancers wailed, trembled, and pushed for security and recognition.

I loved our trip to Montpellier, and the wild journey that followed, but I don't think my mother was able to see the full impact of our expeditions through my pre-teen stonewalling. The joy I felt was a love and

---

5   *Shelter,* written and directed by Jawole Willa Jo Zollar, Laurie Carlos, and hattie gossett, music by Craig Harris, perf. Urban Bush Women et al. Performance, 1988.

appreciation for new places, regular embraces from company members, and the delicious impressions the food and landscapes left on me. On the other hand, the day to day could be tedious or just boring—wake up, eat breakfast, go to warmup, start rehearsals, lunch break, watch rehearsal, have dinner, repeat. And it wasn't just the schedule, but also the expectation to behave, follow the plan, and never deviate. Mealtimes and breaks were my chance to unleash my inner chatterbox and let her fly.

Always invested in my growth, my mom made me take dance classes with the company, which I loathed and resented with every tendu and plie. Pouting, with shoulders hunched, I made it very clear that I was against this daily ritual. As I pointed and flexed my toes, I fired imaginary pellets at my mom. I didn't want to be a dancer. Dancing was too much work, I thought. I wanted to sing. I wanted to write. (Until my sophomore year in college, when I wanted to dance again!)

But back then, I wanted to sit, play, and daydream. My mom insisted I do otherwise, and when either of my parents insisted, I listened. Despite the unwanted dance training, I loved being in France. I loved the food! I loved walking around the city. I loved the overall newness within the safety of the Urban Bush Women. And that newness didn't end with France.

My mom had planned a vacation for the two of us after the tour was over. Most dancers would take the opportunity to do personal traveling after performing in a foreign country. Since we were already in France, it was easy enough for us to take a vacation to another European country. My mom wanted to travel to Spain, specifically Formentera. Our neighbor in New York and my mom's friend, Zoe, had connected her with an affordable place for us to stay.

In order to get there, we had to take a train through Europe, and then a boat. Traveling as a duo—as opposed to traveling with the entire dance company—was much less thrilling for an only child. When it was just the two of us, the banter, gossip, and laughter was reduced to small conversation and parental instruction. I'm sure that it was a welcome break for my mom after weeks of touring with the same people. But for me, I appreciated the colorful personalities, stories, flattery, grooming, and hugs I received from my dance family.

When we were in France, we were in my mom's linguistic domain, as she had been studying French and loved it. While she wasn't fluent, she had been in her comfort zone. However, when it came to traveling to Spain, my mom didn't speak a lick of Spanish, apart from *hola, gracias,* and *por favor.* But, language, just like money, couldn't stop my mom. Secretly, a part of me sometimes wished that it did. Seeing her trying to figure out directions and sort train and boat tickets, with only me as a translator, wasn't very reassuring. It made me nervous. How would she know if this was really the right train? How were we going to find our house? I hated the uncertainty of those situations. My mom had no hesitation when it came to adventure, though—her determination and bohemian nature allowed difficulty to roll off her back—unlike me.

Spain was beautiful, but, like many places in Europe, I didn't see many Black people there. It was just the two of us—a single Black woman and her pre-teen daughter journeying through the European railways to get to Southern Spain. My mom never seemed to worry, or at least, she never allowed her concern to get in the way of our plans. She would push through challenging times and uncomfortable situations to get to where she wanted to be. We traveled lightly by eating sandwiches, saving leftovers, or grabbing affordable yet filling foods, like cheese, tomatoes, and fresh fruit—swaddling it in napkins until our hunger called. Regardless of the circumstances, mom knew how to satisfy our bellies at night, and how to fill our sights during the day.

Finally, after a plane to France, then a train, and finally, a boat, we arrived on the island of Formentera. There were no cell phones back then, so we found a public phone, and my mother managed a phone conversation with the people at the home where we were staying. I can only imagine what that conversation must have been like, without hand gestures and facial expressions to read. My mom gathered directions and we made our way to the house. As luck would have it, there was another issue when we arrived. The owners whom my mom had originally connected with were out of town.

Lost in translation, I waited to discover our fate. The woman my mother was speaking to, out of the kindness of her heart, offered us a room at their property. It wasn't very large, but it was enough for the two of us—all we needed was a bed and a bathroom. They loaned us a hot plate and helped us with provisions. Each morning of our stay, the woman brought us fresh eggs—a natural wonder for this city kid—accompanied by a bottle of freshly pressed olive oil and sweet, rosy tomatoes.

Each day we had the same routine—wash up, eat breakfast, and make our way to the beach. The beaches were some distance away, so we had to plan to be out for a while. The coast of Formentera is made up of beautiful stretches of white, fine sands decorated with nude sun bathers—which I was not accustomed to seeing, being from the States. In France, I had seen women sunbathe topless, but in Formentera, even the men let their private parts swing freely. It was a little more than I asked for, but I couldn't let that stop me from one of my favorite things—hours upon hours of playing and singing at the beach. My mom didn't know how to swim at the time, so I was the official swimmer and Spanish speaker. Nothing fancy—just enough skills to get out of the water and stay afloat.

The beaches in Formentera stretched between multiple islands that were separated by small lakes and pools of water. You could walk from beach to beach, passing through wide gaps between the land, where the ocean would spill through, and then the land would continue. One day, we went swimming and stayed a bit later than usual, and when we wanted to leave, the water between the islands had risen higher than we could stand. I could swim, but my mom couldn't. I paddled my body across, but I could hear my mom gulping and choking behind me. There was no way for me to help her. I wasn't strong enough to swim and pull her at the same time, but I could feel her panic. In fact, it was hard to distinguish her panic from my own.

She eventually made it across with the help of a stranger. I'm sure her conviction to get to me helped her push through whatever fears she faced while swallowing sea water. It didn't help that we lost our way getting home that day, as well. My mom and I got turned around, and instead of our snappy commute, we wound up walking for what felt like hours in the hot, blazing sun—skin salty and sticky, as I hid my fury by listening to my Walkman. After that day, my patience with both the island and my mom diminished.

Yet, within the walls of our little shed, I still came to love Spain. Despite the barriers of language and the challenges of water safety, something wholesome and peaceful made its way into my heart. Our daily eggs, tomatoes, bread, and fresh olive oil, and the various ways my mother's imagination was able to serve them to us, again and again, without me ever getting bored of it. Love had come in and swaddled us, just like the napkins we used to carry our provisions throughout our travels. My mother's tenacity and vision had come through as usual, giving us an unforeseen, fully enriching experience. My fears hadn't been completely laid to rest, as she would surely endeavor upon other risky adventures in the future, but I returned home with something new—memories a photo couldn't capture, shelter off the coast of Spain.

HOW THE DOING GETS DONE

You can change or recreate an entire world in the midst of
Free time
In the midst of long drives
Picking flowers
Or folding laundry
Magic is made
Magic
In nothingness
(Digging down under)
Pitter Patter Putter
Magic is made
In small moments
In small bites
And wishes
In between sponge strokes
And dusting offs
While organizing spices
Waiting for water to boil
And chopping carrots
On walks to nowhere
And long baths
In between pulls of cigarettes
Where there are
No timelines
No appointments
Meetings

Or calls
No schedules
Magic is made
Magic
While watering plants
In the morning
And bathing in the afternoon sunlight
Free time is equal to twice a week's pay
In the midst of napping
Braiding hair
And wiping window sills
The glitter settles
Questions are answered
And ideas bloom into space

Ancestral Connection

VOICE LOG #19

What happens to the voices of a people when they are
choked and lynched to death for over four hundred years?

FRUIT TREE

I swallowed a pit
A pit stuck inside my throat
Maybe it will be a peach one day
Or a plum
For now it remains a moan and a hum

I swallowed a pit
A sour something leaks into my gut
Lies they told
Mistruths to make me a mut

I swallowed a pit
And now my belly swells
A great big tree
I'll birth and bear more cells

I swallowed a pit
And it numbs my tongue
Gnaws at my soul
Which you wish undone

I swallowed a pit
A pit became me
Beautiful fruit
Your rope straining our tree

I swallowed a pit
A pit stuck inside my throat
Maybe it will be a song
With words that we finally wrote

I swallowed a pit
Sometimes it's hard to laugh
And harder to cry
With this choking feeling
Always nearby

UNNAMEABLE MEMORIES

The ship that sailed left me standing
Go tell the rain, it's been falling
The fire spit is still burning
The womb inside which I'm crawling
A lesson longs for the learning
The message left is still calling[6]

My only encounter with an apparition occurred many years ago, after I had been invited to sing in the documentary film *Retour A Goree*.[7] It was the only time I traveled to Africa, and the experience was quite different than I had expected my first visit to be. Instead of vacationing, exploring, or studying, I was working; and much of the time, I was being filmed.

I had been brought to Senegal to sing with a small ensemble of European and American jazz musicians, who had been gathered to present the music of famed Senegalese singer and composer, Youssou N'Dour. The purpose of the project was to connect the roots of Black American music with the music of Senegal via the Middle Passage—traveling from North America and Europe and returning to Senegal. The score of

6 Threadgill, Pyeng. "Safe and Sound." *Portholes To A Love & Other Stories*. Stray Dog Music, 2009.

7 Borgeaud, Pierre-Yves. *Retour à Gorée*. Axiom Films, 2007. 112 minutes. https://www.imdb.com/title/tt0798733/

the film would be woven through Youssou's family legacy in music and storytelling. The film would culminate in an evening length concert of Youssou N'Dour's original music performed by all the musicians and singers in Goree.

Goree is a tiny island off Dakar which once served as a port for enslaved Africans, and it also houses the international landmark museum, *La Maison des Esclaves.* Prior to my visit to Senegal, I had never been to a slave port before. The House of Slaves (as it is known in English) was most active from the years of 1780-1784, and Boubacar Joseph Ndiaye is one of the most well-known people associated with it. As the museum's guide, from 1962 to his death in 2009, Mr. Ndiaye interpreted and translated the history and experiences of the enslaved for most of his life. Just like an artist, he acted as both historian and, arguably, conduit for the many lives and experiences that traveled through that "house."

When I first stepped into the initial holding room where enslaved Africans were first brought, my body was overcome with an overwhelming grief. I could feel the tears of terrified and trapped bodies, waiting in darkness. In my mind, I saw the young and old packed into a space no larger than a small bedroom. We quietly walked through the tiny room, people uncomfortably absorbing the memories of nameless, faceless people. It was apparent that those of us of African descent were having a stronger reaction than our European counterparts. A thread of unnamable memories connected us to imagined stories and real-life experiences. A complicated and conflicted quilt.

Before the tour was over, we were brought to the official separation point, the Door of No Return. I stood still, watching the water calmly lapping at the sides of the building, feeling the architecture imprint a metaphor on my body as it had for thousands of Senegalese and other West African slaves before they arrived in North America, South America, or the Caribbean.

After we visited the museum, there wasn't much conversation amongst us about the impact we felt from visiting the House of Slaves. However, its history, and our reason for performing on Goree Island now held a deeper meaning. The concert on Goree Island was its own kind of process, albeit a stressful one. Despite the moving parts and lack of communication, the magic of the music was undeniable. Performing Youssou's original work for a multi-generational audience of Senegalese fans—for whom Yousou's music and presence is beloved—was infectious. It truly felt as if *we* were the invited guests, and not the other way around.

However, it wasn't until I returned home to my apartment in Berkeley, California, where my husband, daughter, and I were living at the time, that I started to feel the deeper effects of the trip. Coming back across the Atlantic, as my ancestors had done hundreds of years prior—I began to recognize and simultaneously lose track of myself. Like staring down a hall of mirrors, I felt misplaced upon returning home, seeing different angles of my life and body reflected back to me from unfamiliar perspectives. Although I tried to quickly piece myself and my emotions together, I felt conflicted about the parts of me that no longer seemed to fit.

This wasn't entirely surprising, considering the conditions of the film. For much of the project, I had been consumed with learning new music while also keeping up with a highly acclaimed and experienced ensemble and trying to stylistically please an African Pop star—as well as tend to the needs of my own family. I was the youngest performer and the only woman in a group of ten musicians, save for a woman or two on the film crew (whom I rarely had the opportunity to connect with).

Also, it was the longest amount of time I had been away from my daughter, who was just around two years old. Being without her brought its own taste of loneliness, liberation, and longing. Lonely as the only woman performer, liberated to have time alone, and at the same time, longing for a part of myself that it seemed had died, but in fact was transforming into a mother. Goree had birthed a number of unforeseen shifts that would emerge over the next few years.

One of these shifts appeared in the middle of the night. In the middle of a dream, I awoke to see the figure of a man. Tall, thin, and African—he was dressed in a long, beige tunic, pants, and kufi. Although my eyes were open, I was confused and felt a rush of excitement. Ever since a young age, I had been curious about spirits and what it would feel like if I were to see one.

I have had intuitive and empathic suspicions before, that turned out to be true, but never anything quite so visible. Yet that night, as fate would have it, I had the opportunity to see a ghost! But unlike the movies or stories I had overheard from my parents, or watched onscreen, there was nothing eerie about this spirit. He meant me no harm. Although it was the middle of the night, I was eager to soak up the experience—to learn as much from him as I possibly could before he would surely fade away. What was his life work, religion, and story? Was he a family relation? And why had he chosen to come to me?

As much as I yearned for his response, he only shared what his image and presence offered, that he was safe to be around. I had to trust my feelings because he had no voice, and, therefore, no other means of communication. He just stood there, reminding me of his existence, and the doorway I had stood in several weeks before. "I'm with you. I'm part of you," I felt him say.

I had hoped he would bare answers about his life that would unveil truths about my own. There were so many questions erupting in my life at that time, and I desperately needed a guide, but instead what he brought was a reminder that sometimes, at unexpected moments in our lives, the unseen reveals itself to us. *Why* isn't always clear. Perhaps to reassure us that we aren't alone. To let us know that we are, in fact, being watched over. Or perhaps to show us that, as many lives and stories that have been intentionally severed and suffocated, there is a through line. A link. Sometimes the unnamable memories that we feel have faces, bodies, life stories. And one day, in one way or another, they may speak through us when we feel lost—showing us what has always been safe and found.

VOICE LOG #9

I want to be held in the calmness of your
slow focused movements
Patting the wrinkles on my shirt and dress
Let me let myself rest as you've learned to do

YOUR CHANNEL

Your voice reveals a map of you.

Your desires, your fears,
Your ideas, your hopes, your pain,
Your humor,
Your joy, your disappointment,
Your embarrassment, your longing.

But not only YOUR desires and your dreams,
Your fears and loneliness,
Your joy, your hope and your longing,
But those of your grandmothers and grandfathers,
Your aunts and uncles,
Your ancestors
And the next generations to come…
So sing.

AMERICA

Brooklyn, NY. Late afternoon.

A summer afternoon in late July one day in the far off future. An older African-American woman (somewhere in her late 70s) sitting on the front porch reminisces. A familiar face in the neighborhood, she wears an African print handkerchief, gold hoop earrings and white frame glasses while sipping an iced coffee.

LARETHA

Sometimes we have to make up a story 'cause we don't get the whole story given to us, just bits and pieces. B-sides when people tell a story, they always remember it something different, even when they tell the same story over and over again. It repeats, but it also meanders. Jussss like shapeshifters—adding a leg here and an arm there. Suddenly you spot a new tongue or head or a foot—that's storytelling. That's living too. That's what stories do.

I always knew that I had them Native American roots, as well as African people in me. That ain't really news. We all do. There was more roads to my African people, so I could talk with them. Say their names, hold them in regard.

LARETHA nods her head as if gesturing to a congregation

And I wanted to be able to do the same for my Indian blood. This country ain't done right by them either.

I assumed those American Indian people came through my great-grandmother, Grandma Louise. She had those high cheek bones and soft skin that wrinkled into a smile, like silk gathering and being ironed out and gathering back up again. Plus, my Grandma Minnie often said that Grandma Louise's mother (whose name I later discovered, after searching through all kin' of census records) was Phoebe Robinson, and that she the one-part native. I still don't know for sure, but I feel its prolly true. Just ain't got that proof that white folks talk about.

LARETHA purses her lips and keeps talking

See, the funny thing is, I never grabbed the tail of that fish. Caught it, but it slipped right through m'hands! Instead you know what I found out?

LARETHA stops to check that people are listening

What I discovered, what come up from the water, was native people on my mother's side!

My Grandpa Otis was a tough, loud man—so loud I still hear him today, even tho' I never met him. He had chocolate mousse skin, skin so smoothe he make any lady weak in the knees. 'Spose that's what happen when he and Grandma met. But then he mighta surprise her with his broad laugh, and he had those kin'a high ambitions that caused him to push people too often, 'stead of listening. Prolly 'cause he been forced so much in his life too, prolly shocked he didn't break.

That's what this world do to my people. Try to break our pride, sense of safety, ability to trust in each other, and in yourself. But up along his side, if you climb on up the family tree, you see Grandpa Otis had a grandmother named Queen Jones, married to Mr. Price Jones, and that there Queen—she was the daughter of my great-great-great-grandmother, America. Yep, America, jus like this here country. Same one try to tear all us apart, 'cept America was determined to be.

America Sampson married Thomas Sampson. Two of them, I'm told, owned land in Kansas, back when it weren't easy for Black folks t'own land. Not many of us. Hard to procure land and even harder to fin' liberation. And America, as it turns, out was native folk. You know First Nation people. Chawtah.

After some time, I decide start learning something about Chawtah peoples. Find out they all over the Mississippi, them and Chickasaw. That's they land. That's why folks like me fin' them *swimming* all in their blood line. 'Cause they river people. But it ain't always how you think.

   LARETHA pauses intensely for a moment

It ain't always friendly. Sometimes those Chawtah people be taking Black folks for slaves too. Mmm-hmmm, I know. I's surprised too. Make me angry a little, and sad, cause I's wanting us to get along and fight on the same side. Maybe we did, some of us, hopefully we do more in the future.

But that's just how things was, confusing like that, like telling stories. White folks tell a story—it don't sound nothing like when we tell a story. They come here running from hell and pain and bring all that pain right here to this land, never free themselves fully 'fore coming here, and that's why come all these people gotta suffa. Mexican, Japanese, Indian. 'Cause they ain't take care of themselves, have their own family talk. Them is hard to have, but once in a while need to do it. Stop just carrying on like everything's all right...when it's not.

But when I fin' out them names of Mrs. Grandma America and

Grandpa Thomas Sampson, I start celebrating. I always do that. When I'm getting close I gets all excited, can't sleep at night, too, like being in love or standing at the top of a mountain looking down ova' everything. I wake up my husband, sleeping tight next to me. I wake him 'cause I was so excited. I said "I know they names! I know they names!"

"What?" he half asleep and sounding confused. I'm nodding my head.

"I know they names!"

"Who?" he ask, eyes half open.

"My people," I say. "The people in me."

And he say, "That's good," still half-dreaming, letting me 'splain how I found them and who's mommy and daddy is who. He lie there listening a little while and soon he fall back off asleep. But I stayed awake staring at that piece of paper what my granddaughter give me, that one she printed out for me that say America Sampson and have her picture on it.

She's sitting there. Sitting there like she posing for all us family to see.

LARETHA pauses as if looking at them from across the way

Her and Grandpa Thomas in the middle of the land. See the two of them, and he with his eye shut, 'cause a some injury white people made on him for owning too much or knowing too much...or not keeping his mouth closed. They close that eye,

LARETHA tilts her head down to look over her sunglasses for emphasis

But you see he still seeing out both of 'em.

    LARETHA quickly pushes her glasses back

I say, "finally, I got they names and a picture I can see." That's good for me. That's good enough for me.

    Lights fade out.

THE QUEEN OF CAKES

My grandmother made cakes. Lemon, coconut, German chocolate, strawberry shortcake. Every time I say it, I taste them in my mind. The stories of her mixing, and baking, and everyone's enthusiastic mouthfuls savoring her culinary offerings. My father diving into flour bins, her father eating up freshly baked somethings before serving time. I have to use my imagination to smell and taste, the way that I use my imagination to envision the world that I want to exist.

Grandma Lillian made those cakes with ingredients she told me about in ancestral fairytales. Stories of a different time, a different Chicago. A Chicago with streetcars, where men and women pressed their suits and hair to look their best, just to step outside in the blazing sun or blizzarding snow. A time where watermelon always arrived with a song, fresh milk came from the milkman, and butter was creamy, and eggs were, too. A time where ice cream tasted so close to the cream from which it was made, that many in my family nearly ate themselves sick with it. My grandma's shopping list had key ingredients that made their way to her by way of a man in a truck, or on foot, with a song. So, her cakes had songs, too.

Ohhhhh milkman, milkman, milk is here...

People often ask if anyone on my father's side came from music. There was my Aunt Evelyn, Grandma Lillian's sister, who received a scholarship to study opera in college; and there was also the praise, or songs, from the family about those cakes that Grandma baked. In a way, you could say she was indirectly in music. You can't sing *milk* to someone, and then bake a cake or bread, with that same milk, and expect the song not to enter the bread. Cooking, just like music, feeds on love and intention.

I never got to taste Grandma Lillian's pastries, but I inhaled her cake chronicles from both her and my father. Their distinction is faint, but their aroma still lingers in my memory. The image of everyone sitting around the dining table after eating a meal of roast with root vegetables, cooked greens, and freshly baked bread made by my great-grandfather, followed by one of Grandma's cakes.

It's funny, but by the time I came around, Grandma Lillian had mostly stopped baking. I wonder if she had made herself sick with the sweetness of life, just as my father and his uncles had gobbling home-made ice cream? Perhaps my older brother, Melin, got to taste her cakes, but by the time I came around, the most baking Grandma did was making biscuits and her annual fruit cakes, sent at Christmastime. Edible Christmas lights hidden inside all-purpose flour. She indulged us with her biscuits one time, in her later years, when she came to New York to visit after my younger sister, Nhumi, was born. I can see her sitting in the kitchen, patting butter and flour together between her hands, talking us through the recipe as everyone eagerly awaited her cloudy delights.

Grandma Lillian also made lampshades—yes, lampshades. She would sit in her second-tier apartment, the one upstairs from Grandma Pierce, my great-grandmother, her mother, and sew. That home was like a three-layer cake with uneven layers, secret fillings, and humble, but delicious toppings. You wouldn't know it from the outside, but once biting into the center, something would just keep you coming back for more, like I did each summer throughout most of my childhood.

That house on South Sangamon housed my great-grandmother, Grandma Pierce, as we referred to her, my great-uncle, Herbert, her brother, and my great-aunt, Marjorie, her sister. She and my great-grandmother had the two larger apartments, while my great-uncle lived in the basement where the lines of washed laundry hung long and stretched out, like him. You always knew Uncle Herbert was around by the sound of his feet swishing on the floor, like brushes on a snare. I never saw his room, and never really knew much about his private life, either. But he remained a key ingredient of that house, staying on to the end, even after Grandma had to be moved to an assisted living facility.

My great-aunt, Marjorie, lived in a bedroom off to the side of Grandma Lillian's apartment on the second floor. A bedroom that I never saw the insides of, except for the clothes and various odd items—purses, belts, shoes, and hats that she squashed and stuffed behind the door like wild, tropical plants, all fighting to be let out to touch the sun.

Whenever Aunt Marjorie would emerge, it would be late at night, coming or going—from where I didn't know—to give me some gift of funny-smelling perfume or lotion she had come across in her travels through the city, or from cleaning people's homes. Both she and my uncle shared the downstairs kitchen with Grandma Pierce, so you could smell their cooking from time to time.

Aunt Marjorie could always grab your attention with her high-pitched cackle—short legs shooting out from her as she laughed. As collard greens simmered slowly on the stove and the television played, Grandma Pierce would be sitting quietly beside her walker at the dining table, nodding off now and then. All these characters were a feast for my eyes and imagination.

Although she lived in a home with her mother and siblings, it felt as if Grandma Lillian lived a separate life. After climbing the steep stairs and entering her apartment—those stairs that creaked to alert me that Grandma was home—you would arrive in the dining room. The living room was to the right, where many of my summer days were spent watching old tv shows, like *Green Acres*, *Bewitched*, and *Gidget*. Sometimes I would sit with Grandma to watch the shows she liked, such as *Matlock*, *Murder She Wrote*, or *Get Smart*. Grandma Lillian always liked mysteries, but with a side of slapstick comedy—I guess that runs in the family. Mysteries lingered even as she fell asleep at night gossiping with the telephone in her hand, stocking cap molding her hair as the *Green Hornet* played on her small clock radio.

During the day, when Grandma wasn't taking me around to visit family, see fireworks, work her part-time office job, or visit her best friend, Faustine (who would inevitably cook an all-you-can-eat buffet for us), she would sit in her dining room and sew. In the evening (or the morning), wearing her house dress and stocking cap, sometimes leaving her dentures resting on the bathroom sink (her upper lip coyly covering her naked gums when she smiled), Grandma would wind thread around sturdy fabric, so that it would stay fixed to the wire, like muscle to bone. She was like some kind of witch-seamstress, constructing and mending lamps to keep people's homes bright, and perhaps their hearts, as well. I wonder if she ever thought of it that way—that all her sewing was intended to help things stay together, or to keep things from falling apart.

The irony is that—unlike her cakes, those lampshades weren't particularly stunning. People weren't beating down the doors and placing endless orders. She didn't sew them in magnificent yellows or vibrant pinks, they were often muted, off-white tones. More than anything, it was the fabric that stood out. The lines flowing side by side, like a flock of birds. Raw silks and consistent cottons. Endless scraps of rippled fabrics spread on the dining table, held in place by her massive collection of needles and thread.

Even though she was a woman of the fifties, from the outside, it seemed Grandma maintained her expected maternal duties and still found a way to do some of what she pleased. My grandma met my grandfather when she was quite young, maybe 19 or 20. She never said it explicitly, but I imagine Grandpa wooed her pretty good with his city-slicker, high-rolling charm. Grandpa Floyd, or Rico, as people referred to him, was tall, thin, and handsome. Fair-skinned, fine-haired, and always dapper, especially in his youth. But he was on a solo mission with assignments specially focused on his needs.

Grandma Lillian said that when she got pregnant, she decided to move down to Arkansas or Alabama—wherever it was that Grandpa was stationed with the Army at the time. Being the oldest of ten, and quite independent, she packed herself up and made her way to go live with Grandpa Rico. However, it didn't take her very long to realize that Grandpa had a wandering eye. Grandma had too much self-pride to endure his womanizing and decided early on that she would need a different kind of marital arrangement. So, they divorced and she raised my dad and Aunt Carol at home with her mother, grandfather, and other relatives.

I don't know how things were before I was born, but when I came along, Grandma was always on amicable terms with Grandpa. Every summer, she arranged for me to visit relatives and he was always on the list. We would visit Grandpa Rico at his house, where he lived with his aunt, my great-aunt, Odie. I loved visiting them and shuffling through Grandpa's drawer full of old photos, sitting like loose playing cards waiting to be sorted. Grandpa had been a gambler his entire life—setting up game rooms for the Italian mafia and doing other related jobs.

When we would get to his house, he would either be returning from his favorite bar, where he liked to socialize, or sitting with his legs folded over the arm of his couch. It was always funny to see an elderly man lying on the couch like a kid, except in his case, there was no one there to reprimand him. Grandpa lived life by his own rules. Grandma would give me her signature smirk as Grandpa started one of his old-man rants. She never argued with him—she would just give that look that said "to each his own," while Aunt Odie would sit in her bedroom complaining about something he had done.

They may have gotten on each other's last nerve, but for me, it was all a joy. Their frustration, their under-the-breath commentary, and their crumpled faces tickled me more than anything. I guess, because, through it all, I knew that they loved me. I could see it in their eyes when I walked in the room, in their kisses on my cheeks, in the warm linger of their hugs, and in the random gifts they handed me. I just felt loved, so their bickering never mattered.

Families require a lot of pins to stay together. And still, we don't stay together as imagined. Sometimes we're hanging by a thread, but now I recognize that's still an accomplishment, considering all that life doles out. Those people and connections, or lack thereof, are the fabric of who we are.

The last time I saw my grandma was in the hospital, about a month before she died. My daughter and I flew to Chicago to visit her. My dad, my younger sister, my stepmother, and her sister were all there, along with my great-uncle, Cleveland and his wife, Auntie Gloria, and one of my dad's cousins. I remember Grandma lying on that narrow hospital bed. She was smaller than I had ever known her to be, and stiffer in body and mind. Her eye color had faded, too.

Because of her ailments, she wasn't allowed to eat anything except for chipped ice. Toward the end of our visit, she started mumbling something. My younger sister, Nhumi, and I leaned in to hear what it was, thinking she had an urgent request. She repeated herself, speaking loud enough for us to comprehend. "You know what I wish? I wish I could just have a sweet roll," she said.

I started laughing. I thought to myself, "Here's Grandma, at the end of her days, and she's still thinking about cake."

A HIDDEN POWER

Imagine yourself as a child, sitting in your room. Your little legs and arms are dangling and moving about, the way that children continuously shuffle, so full of energy, ready for the world. What if each morning and evening, instead of a bedtime story, you were lulled and awakened with the names of your grandmothers and grandfathers? Spoken to you over and over, like waves connecting with the shore, rhythmically brushing the soles of your feet, and reminding you from where you came. Imagine how that might shape you, if it were repeated to you from the time of your birth, like your times tables or the alphabet.

Over and over, names drawing every inch and crevice of your family tree into your memory. Spelling out the will, wit, stubbornness, and courage of your ancestors. Their ingenuity, their beauty, their shame, their struggle, their perseverance, their power. When I think of the people I come from, I feel powerful. I think of their slow and steady, unapologetic power—unwilling to be pushed down.

All my life I felt as if I were being watched over, despite being an only child—protected by an invisible blanket of people. I suppose that feeling first came to me as a young child, growing up amongst a large community of artists. It was reinforced by my large extended family. During summer visits, when I would go to see relatives in Chicago, Georgia, and California, it wasn't uncommon for me to meet a new aunt, uncle, or cousin. So I grew up with the expectation of meeting new family, because my family was that big, I thought. It was as if there were an invisible thread connecting me to others and safeguarding me wherever I went.

The stories from my paternal grandmother enhanced that bond.

Stories about my great-aunts and uncles, my great-grandmother, and the childhood tales of my mischievous father became their own kind of legend. Years later, in college, it became part of the inspiration that led me to research my family tree. However, I had no idea at the time that the theme of family history would return to me twenty years later through my own music and songwriting.

When I first began researching and writing the music for my album, *Head Full of Hair, Heart Full of Song,* I became deeply immersed in learning about the early traditions of Black hair care. Having had natural hair all my life, it was something I took for granted. It wasn't until my thirties that I started to notice a larger movement towards natural hair in Black communities. So much so that even my white husband would remark on how often he saw Black women wearing their hair in natural hairstyles. I started to realize that Black identity, beauty, and culture vis-à-vis hair was a theme close to my heart.

I wanted to learn more about the history of hair. The plants, oils, herbs, clays, and butters Africans brought to the United States to protect their hair and bodies from the literal and figurative blows of slavery and racism. I began to study the elaborate hairstyles that African women wove and what they signified—the way that one hairdo could symbolize a woman's readiness to marry, while another might mean that she was a widow. The way in which African women wove seeds into their hair, like black-eyed peas, to propagate on new soil.

Slavery placed deep scars, not only upon our bodies and minds, but also upon our tresses, impacting our views of one another and ourselves. Growing up with natural hair, I was familiar with the positive and negative attention I might receive whenever my hair wasn't tamed in braids or twists. I felt it in the comments Black folks made to one another about our "nappy edges," or the biased comments that people of all backgrounds made about hair texture.

Whose hair was *beautiful,* and why? The way that some Black men praised me when I had locs or wore an Afro, while other Black men would avert their eyes or barely look my way. As a teenager, the comments white friends made when they'd find lost strands of my hair, like, "Is that pubic hair?" insinuating an "uncleanliness" to my natural hair. One lyric—"got a head full of hair and a heart full of song"—had begotten an entire treasure trove of questions, and also an abandoned pile of invisible bruises.

Before the transatlantic slave trade, Africans had easy access to shea butter, red clay, and other humectants to moisturize and protect their scalps and hair, so that it would grow strong and healthy. They made combs specifically carved for the thickness and curliness of our hair. They had the appropriate amount of time set aside to wash and braid one another's hair, honoring laughter and storytelling as part of the process. And even when there wasn't an abundance of time or money for these rituals, there was still a collective appreciation for our hair.

When Africans arrived on this shore in bondage, they were denied these seemingly basic, yet significant, connections to their traditions and culture. Over time, we devised ways to care for ourselves, and our hair, again. Bit by bit, through trial and error, replacing lard and brutalizing sheep shears with gentler herbal solutions. Stealing away time for our hair meant stealing away time for ourselves, gradually rebuilding spaces to tend to our wounds, beauty, and dreams.

Combing through texts and films, I started to see the entanglement between our physical bodies and the world around us, our strength, and our vulnerability. Our hair, pride, traditions, and our lineage. Our true texture. Initially, I thought that this would be sufficient for my project— hair and ancestry. I began writing music about ancestry, and that, together with several songs, unveiled the profound depth and symbolism of hair. Black hair was as deep as the roots of our collective family tree, and thick with metaphor and life lessons.

But then I realized that hair wasn't enough. It was only a portion of the ingredients vital to our self-celebration. As I picked up the brush to unravel hair, I realized I couldn't separate hair from our bodies, nor our faces. I started to reflect on the Black women that I grew up with; dancers like Pat Hall Smith and Viola Sheeley. Hair and beauty whisperers in beauty shops, self-made entrepreneurs, single mothers twisting and braiding new positions for themselves. Poet authors, like hattie gossett and Ntozake Shange, bedazzling themselves with crystals and piercings, shimmering and shocking us awake, just like their words. Their energy radiated through me in my early teenage years and has lasted to the present.

Black women don't just do their hair and go. For us, getting dressed is an act of self-anointing, a blessing. With this here blue wig, blond dreadlocks, cornrows, fade—I anoint myself. With these hoops, door-knockers, beads—I celebrate myself. And with this fuchsia, fire-engine red, aubergine lipstick—I claim my sensuality and the power of my words.

Every moment a Black woman chooses to wrap herself in a neck-lace, paint her face, accentuate her breasts or hips, is a moment where she creates a space to honor herself and her beauty. It's a moment when she can transform the ideology, image, and language of a warped culture that tells Black women and girls that there is something inherently wrong with them, something that needs to be flattened, fixed, straightened, lightened, fastened.

It was at this point in my research that I started to become infatuated with adornment. There are innumerable ways in which African diasporic people have and continue to decorate themselves. In the midst of this glorious fascination and reclamation, I came upon an artist named Laolu Senbanjo, or Laolu, as he is known. Laulo is a Nigerian artist and musician who paints on sneakers, t-shirts, jackets, pants, bodies, and anything else he is inspired to create upon. The intention behind his drawing is to share his Yoruba culture through living, visual prints.

I don't know where I first discovered Laolu, but once I found him, I became extremely taken with his work. Here was a contemporary Nigerian artist using ancestral traditions and mythology in street art. It was the new-old remix so common in Black art, just like jazz or hip-hop. It reminded me of the books I had collected on the Surma, Karo, and Maasai and their traditional chalk and ochre markings. Laolu was doing something similar yet updated.

Laulo's work excited me because it upheld the significance of symbolism in fashion and imagery for Black diasporic people. One day, in the Spring of 2016, I discovered that Laulo was going to be giving a talk at the Brooklyn-based Museum of Contemporary African Diasporan Arts, MoCADA. I immediately bought tickets for my husband and I, and told several close friends who also happened to be visual artists. What most excited me about the event was that Laulo would be doing a live demonstration of his process.

My husband and I arrived at MoCADA early and I sat in my seat, tingling with anticipation. Laulo arrived and began his talk. During his lecture, he spoke about his life growing up in Nigeria. He initially started working as a lawyer—a good job, which pleased his parents and the rest of his family. However, while the social justice causes which he fought for at work inspired him, being a lawyer did not. He felt he wasn't living his true calling. So, one day, on a whim, he decided to quit being a lawyer, took a leap of faith, and became an artist. He moved to New York and his adventures in art-making began.

Laolu also spoke of the influences throughout his childhood in Nigeria. As a young boy, his grandmother would recite the names of all his ancestors to him. Over and over, she said the names of his grandmothers and grandfathers, regularly activating their strength within him like a magic tonic.

Laulo calls his work "The Sacred Art of the Ori." In Yoruba, one of the languages (and groups of people) of Nigeria, *ori* is a word used to refer to one's literal head, and the place where one's spiritual intuition and destiny is said to sit. When Laulo works on people, he often uses white paint, sometimes black, to draw on the nude body or face of the subject. He describes his process as one of intuiting, or sensing, the person whom he is working on. He then crafts their insides on the outside. It is both a mask and a revealing. The symbols and style of drawing Laulo uses relate to the Yoruba myths of his childhood.

In comic books, cartoons, and superhero movies, we try to create super humans by imbuing them with exceptional powers, such as the ability to fly, create storms, or spontaneously make fire. Over four hundred years ago, enslaved Africans arrived on these shores with a multitude of methods for making sense of some of the most horrific life circumstances. We survived the gruesome and inhumane. Yet we have magical messages flickering in our hair, style, social dances, and cultural swagger. Our ancestors are the wings which we seek in order to fly.

PLENTY SONG TOO

Savannah, Georgia. Midday.

An enslaved African woman of medium height stands barefoot cleaning an elaborate dining table where lunch has just been served. Although her face appears old, her body is strong and still youthful. Dressed in an old apron tied over tattered clothes, her hair is half covered, and she glistens with perspiration from the Southern heat.

SABLE

Mah heart beat like I be'n runnin'. Runnin' all day, every day. I hear mah heart go fast. Sometimes too loud to hear massa voice, loud in mah ears, loud in mah head. Sweatin' all day. Washin', ironin'. Pickin' cotton, pullin' cotton, straigh'en cotton.

Mah skin hurt, legs, feet, too. No one want to look at me but massa and dem they made me like dis. I know I's pretty underneath.

SABLE pauses and then speaks as if talking to herself

I know I's pretty.

No time for mah self. No washin', ironin', foldin'.

No soap. No smellin' good. Massa say it nah righ' how we smell,

SABLE speaks growing more and more agitated

but it nah righ' if we smell good too. We have to wash when massa say. Have to eat when massa wife say. When dey done with de food, we get whas left. When dey trow it away, we get clothes, maybe shoes, table for bread. When dey animals stink an' piss too many times, den we get dey mat to sleep on.

We play and dance when dey ain't lookin'.

Make sure dey ain't lookin'.

We got clothes torn and feet bleedin' and scars dat don't have time to heal. Skin burnt and tough like dried meat. More dan we eat. Torn from thorns and bushes and whips and I got a head dat aches me. Aches me cause mah babies, dey want to suckle and de men do too. Dey want more sweetness jus' like de babies do. Want to forget de ways of being men, but I got ideas.

SABLE touches her head as if to ease a pain

Mah head aches 'cause I got ideas dat no one wants but me...even I don't want dem sometimes. Mah head hurts. I rather lay dem to rest like children born still, tired at de breast because all mah milk done sucked from massa's babies.

I see pictures in mah head, pictures I like to paint on da wall with color, something like what massa got in he room. I got words dat I want to put in un of dem books like what massa got in dat library he always sit in, reading late at night. De un room he don't let massa wife go to. But I see her wantin' to go in.

She sneak in jus' like Tommy try sneakin' 'way, 'cept he never come back askin' me and sister fren' to tell if massa come by. He jus keep runnin'.

I got songs too.

Songs betta than those songs massa wife and him sing at little Abigail's birthday, better than dem songs dey sing on sundays and after dem parties. Parties we make fuh dem.

I got songs. I got sad songs and happy 'uns too. Will'm say I's a good singer.

SABLE smiles to herself

Likes it when I sing him to sleep. Sometimes he ask me even when de baby already sleep just cuz he like de sound of mah voice. He say I's pretty underneath too. Underneath all dem beatins. He say I's pretty. I can't see it. Cause I don't never got de time to see me. No times for de ideas in mah head. Only that 'un time when I look past de mirror and dat like looking at a bad dream. Who dat old woman staring at me? It happen that 'un time when I look in massa's wife bedroom, cleaning her pot and fixing her clothes and hair do I see what I look like. How come dem wan' me looking like dat?

SABLE stops cleaning

Massa cover my face so and push 'tween mah legs, push so hard til I have no voice and he moan like he took mine. Take mah voice, make mah voice crack every time I speak...so I can't even sing mah baby to sleep. Can't hardly whisper a prayer, just have to think it in mah head. Make sure dey ain't lookin'.

Can't even sing mah self to sleep. Cus no sound come out at first, but den by 'n by, time pass I find it again. And when I do, mah baby she smile some, start eatin', g'ttin' fat, mah breast start come full and I have enough milk for mah baby and massa baby too. And massa stop looking at me fuh now 'cause he don't wan' to be around so many babies, even do he de 'un make dem.

I got all dese ideas. Heart beat like I be'n runnin'. All kinda ideas I see. Wanna put dem up on a wall like what massa got in dey eatin' room, bedroom too. I got ideas fuh all dem books massa read. I got pages and pages a story, an plenty song too.

Black out

The Voice Erotic

VOICE LOG #17

I never knew my voice and my vulva had so much meaning.

THE VOICE EROTIC

"Eroticism is a quality that causes sexual feelings, as well as a philosophical contemplation concerning the aesthetics of sexual desire, sensuality, and romantic love. That quality may be found in any form of artwork, including painting, sculpture, photography, drama, film, music, or literature.[8]"

Laboring women exhale low and deep to open their wombs
Their voices directing blood and tissue which way to go
To stretch, lengthen, widen, soften
Stretch, strengthen, protect
Descending pitches spiraling
Through spinal columns
Moving and reverberating
Down down down
Altering two bodies at once
Moaning life into existence

The infinite call and response
Echoing between rolling figures
On a bed,
Meadow,
Floor,

---

8   Wikipedia contributors, "Eroticism," Wikipedia, The Free Encyclopedia, https://en.wikipedia.org/w/index.php?title=Eroticism&oldid=1156225717 (accessed May 23, 2023).

Hotel room,
Seashore
Sound and movement converge
As bassy desires pour out
Reshaping torsos, pelvis and limbs
Through panting and perspiration
Tears and exclamation
Sound creates form
Altering two bodies at once

Love perspires
From sensuous sunshine
and saline waters
From sweaty dance floors
and cleansing rains
From fruit on the verge of bursting
and desert canyons
From effortless laughter
and tropical flora
To the jungle inside of you
Constantly reconfiguring
Opening the depths of space in your chest
Exposing lungs
Grief and gratitude
That open and close
Like butterflies' wings
Releasing
Hardened chests
Hardened faces
To stretch, lengthen, widen, soften

Such unapologetic self-enjoyment is contagious
Catching like a melody

Bouncing from form to form
Like orgasmic airwaves
Humming into your blood and bones
Renewing you again

The cascade of living
Intersecting with your abdomen
and exiting your mouth
Moving through your thoughts
and extending out your genitals
Rushing into your heart
and rippling out your fingers
Grasping for memories of softness
Forgiveness,
Love
Heat
Stillness

Flashes of lightning
and darkness
Resuscitating you again
Feeling sprouting in the dead parts
Where you thought there was no more life

Your voice
Helps cells to regenerate
Grow and multiply
Like a newborn
Finding their lungs for the first time

THE LAND SINGS

"A species smaller than the eye can see
Or larger than most living things
And yet we take from them without consent
Our shelter, food, habiliment
But who am I to doubt or question the inevitable being
For these are but a few discoveries we find inside
the secret life of plants.[9]"

—STEVIE WONDER

Sometime between 2008 and 2009, I began writing music for a new project—a song cycle entitled *Songlines: Singing The Land.* The idea was based on songlines, an Aboriginal belief and tradition, that in order to travel from one place to the next, one must use an inherited oral history shared in the form of song, chant, prayer, and movement. Through each song and/or movement, a shaman, medicine person, or spiritual guide would pass on the knowledge of the land.

Many cultural traditions have created this type of compositional map, from Aboriginal to African American. An Aboriginal version of "Follow the Drinking Gourd" to get from point A to B, plant life to water, and better understand nature without being harmed or harming it. When I first learned about songlines, a number of ideas, questions,

---

9   Stevie Wonder. "The Secret Life of Plants." *Journey Through the Secret Life of Plants.* Motown Records, 1979.

and theories raced through my brain. I couldn't help but wonder what my relationship to the natural world would be like if I had been taught to see and hear the trees, the grass, the mountains, and the rivers in this way. I set about researching and writing songs for the collection following these initial questions.

The first song I wrote was titled "Songlines." It was an ode to the original concept of indigenous people and Black people living close to nature, but also to mourning our severed connections to the land, as well as our ancestors. "She Lives with the Sun" was one of the next songs I wrote. This song similarly expresses a push and pull, but the push and pull of motherhood and being an artist. While basking in the beauty of your shining child, your heart grows; and, yet, as an artist, there is a part of you always missing your connection to your artistic practice.

The songs continued to write themselves in this way. A kind of dialogue and commentary on the land outside, and the inner landscape of being human, particularly, a Black human. *Songlines* was the first project where I allowed myself to vent about the larger world's ignorance and denial of African diasporic and indigenous genius. I discovered I had a lot to say and a lot of feelings as well.

From the transatlantic Slave Trade to the Great Migration, from the terror of lynchings to redlining, and so much more, these experiences have dramatically changed our relationship with the natural world. In 2022, many Black Americans live in cities, and many don't own a home for various reasons—often linked to systemic oppression. For some communities or families where there has been home and land ownership, we have had our homes and land taken away by the government or large development corporations. And there is an added sting when farmers markets, health food stores, grocery chains, and farm-to-table restaurants often brand themselves as spaces primarily suited for middle- or upper-class people.

First Nation people and enslaved Africans brought most, if not all, of our planting, farming, and herbal wisdom to this country. Our wisdom and muscle. We built agricultural systems for lucrative crops like sugar, indigo, cotton, tobacco, and coffee, which have become the backbone of wealth for white American families and America, at large. Yet, in our communities, many young Black children don't have ties to that wealth and have never planted or picked their own food.

In 2010, as part of my research, I attended the first annual Black Farmers & Urban Gardeners Conference in Brooklyn. I think I was the only person who wasn't a part of a community garden, or a farmer, or a food justice activist, but it was no less gratifying or invigorating to feel the passion of a group of Black folks gathered to talk about the potentiality of gardens. Then I learned many Black farmers experience higher incidence rates of discrimination from government policies, making it increasingly difficult to make a living.

I was accustomed to thinking of all farmers as having a hard time succeeding, but I didn't realize that many of the farmers I often heard about were white farmers, and that they were perpetuating the same kinds of white terrorist actions already at play throughout our country. I also heard positive accounts of the socio-psychological impacts that gardens have on relationships.

Will Allen—former basketball player, keynote speaker, and founder of Growing Power, an urban agriculture organization started in Milwaukee, WI—established his non-profit in order to teach city-dwellers how to build their own urban gardens. Allen has taught many growers around the country how to make good quality compost for healthy soil, and how to plant vegetables, and even how to breed tilapia. In his talk, he placed particular emphasis on the impact that a garden can create in a high-crime neighborhood, replacing empty lots. Through his own work transforming abandoned lots into gardens, crime rates went down, people felt a sense of pride in their surroundings, and greater trust and connection started to emerge in the community.

The implications of gardening were profound to me, but I was just a singer/songwriter. If only I could communicate the power of the work these folks were doing. I had dreams of performing my song cycle at community gardens and multi-purpose community centers around the country. But the realities of being an independent artist made this too difficult to fully actualize. Instead, the music remained unrecorded and mostly unknown.

However, thanks to the digital landscape, some of the representation of farming and organic lifestyles has broadened. Instead of just farm-to-table and organic eateries being depicted as white families or gatherings of white hipsters eating delicious, nourishing fruits and vegetables, now we see Black and brown people forging themselves into the vision of fertile land. Social media handles like "Black Girls with Gardens" and "Botanical Black Girl" are growing. Social justice farming and plant educators like Leah Penniman of Soul Fire Farm, and singer and chef Kelis of Bounty and Full are expanding the visibility of Black Americans and the American farm landscape. Thanks to podcasts, social media trends, and other affordable systems of marketing, more Black people are having a resurgence in farming and environmentally conscious spaces.

In fleeing the south, and the horrors and trauma of slavery, many of us also became distanced from our own cultural traditions and wisdom. The soil contains a complex web of opposing memories. Our safety, whether in nature or in urban environments, has been severely at risk since 1619, when the first Africans were brought here in chains, and Turtle Island became America. But little by little, the voices of leading gardeners like Ron Finley, aka the Gangsta Gardener, and food writers such as Stephen Satterfield of *High on the Hog*, are helping to restore our songlines again.

The other night I watched the documentary *Muscle Shoals*[10], about the groundbreaking recording studio in Muscle Shoals, Alabama, where countless hit songs have emerged. There again I saw the silhouette of our chart home—from Aretha Franklin's "I Never Loved a Man," to The Staple Singers' "I'll Take you There," to Wilson Picket's "Mustang Sally." In the beginning of the film, one musician after another confessed their

---

10   Camalier, Greg. *Muscle Shoals*. Magnolia Pictures, 2013. 111 minutes. https://www.imdb.com/title/tt2492916/

bewilderment at how such an unglamorous place in the middle of no-where could birth so much beautiful music. I instantly shouted, "It's the land! The land is singing!"

BECOMING EMBODIED

"I'm a girl from a cotton field! That pulled myself above what was not taught to me. And I question myself and say, 'How can you say you deserve a well-to-do family when you are with this body, when you came from the cotton fields, when you came from the family that you came from? And when you came from all of the destruction and the mistakes?' Because I want more, simply because I want more. Look what I have done in this lifetime, with this body.[11]"

—TINA TURNER

Ever since I was in high school I was interested in meditation and movement. My mom says that I asked her to help me find a Yoga class and soon began studying with other grownups in my spare time. By the time I was in college I started a meditation group and became certified in Reiki with a spiritual mentor. Something always intrigued me about Yoga, Qi-Gong, and other Somatic practices, although I never knew where it would lead me.

I started teaching private voice lessons when we lived in Berkeley, California. I had no idea what I was teaching then. I didn't even know how I knew what I knew. I just thought of myself as goofy, like a Tracee Ellis Ross but without the hit TV shows and stunning wardrobe. My husband would laugh at me when I spontaneously created songs around the house, or busted into impersonations of someone we had just met.

---

11   Lindsay, Daniel, and Martin, T.J. *Tina*. HBO, 2021. 118 minutes.
        https://www.hbo.com/movies/tina

He'd say, "It's all so natural to you. But you know not everyone grew up the way you did, right? It's not that simple for everyone else."

It took years for me to really digest his words. I worked with many students, of all ages, and noticed how often people seemed disconnected from their sense of playfulness and innate creativity. Growing up around creative, improvised music and dance—that's one thing you never lose, that sense of play. It stays with you, as if it's in the water. But translating it for others is another thing. Most people are quick to stop their flow of ideas just as soon as they start to pour out from the faucet of their imagination. In teaching voice, I had to learn not only how to help people to understand their vocal mechanism, but also their larger physical body, to integrate the two, and express themselves authentically.

In the fall of 2014, I finally gathered the guts and curiosity to begin my first Embodied Voice class on a weekly basis. At the time, I hadn't heard of vocalist/composer Lisa Sokolov's Embodied Voice technique, but she had been teaching it for several decades. I just knew that I wanted to offer an opportunity to interested and passionate people to expand and explore the full range of their voices in connection with their bodies. I also wanted to run something that was affordable and consistent, so that other people could experience some of the not so subtle somatic awakenings that I had been experiencing for some time.

I realized that not everyone was going to want to become a certified Alexander Technique teacher, nor was everyone going to become a Somatic Voicework™ teacher. Still, I wanted to deliver something potent, using those methods, for everyday people, aspiring artists, and singer-songwriters. How could I offer them a way to gradually heighten their sensitivity and awareness to the vast possibilities of the voice and body? How could I offer a framework that would help people experience the mirroring between their bodies, how they breathe, move, and the sounds they produce?

I found a lovely, intimate studio in my neighborhood, just two blocks from my house. It was beautifully decorated and situated within the brownstone of a bodyworker and former dancer. The space had dark wood floors and high ceilings, and would comfortably fit eight to ten people for a yoga class. Since we would be making sounds and moving around, it would be best for a total of six or eight people. I developed a structure for teaching class, and then, all I needed was to find interested participants.

I thought about how amazing it would be to offer a group class for people to journey together, week after week. For years during my Alexander Technique training at the Balance Arts Center, I had explored nuanced patterns—such as the subtle movements of my tongue—as I swallowed, inhaled, or sang. As a singer, wind, or even brass player, the habits of your tongue can have a dramatic effect on your tone.

In sensing the width of the back of my tongue, I discovered that tension in my neck and shoulders would release. I learned how the muscles in my upper back were inclined to take over when I went to lift my arms or move my legs. I found that through sensing my eyes as three dimensional, not just flat surfaces to see from, that my chest opened and helped me to feel the full width of my feet on the floor. I simultaneously began to find strength and connection, like nothing else, by regularly focusing on my lower back, and noticing how it related to my middle and upper back in all activities. It was difficult to convey the full impact of these things in only one hour—or one class, or just in words—without someone experiencing it for themselves.

I really looked forward to sharing these ideas in my new voice class. I wondered if my students would uncover new connections between their voices and bodies that I hadn't yet experienced. Would they find space where previously there had been constriction? Would they unlock greater power from their voices and bodies, leading to more confidence?

Sadly, I would never find out the answers to these questions. As any independent artist, yoga teacher or musician knows, growing and maintaining a regular class or following in New York City is one of the hardest things to accomplish. It would have been easier to build a crowd busking in Union Square.

In the first week of teaching my Embodied Voice class, I had only three students—one of whom was usually a friend—and I don't think I ever got over that number. Some weeks I had just one student—other times, none. In the colder months, when students were less likely to confirm with me beforehand, I let my winter nesting get the best of me. I eventually gave up on the weekly class idea. Like so many of my passion projects, no matter how enthusiastic I was, or how much wealth of information I had to share, it would still take more than that to draw people in on a consistent basis.

The times in which people did attend, I got a taste of how voice and movement work affected others—especially people who didn't consider themselves professional singers. This became the seed to understanding how strongly people want to connect with their voices. As for the professional singers, my class provided them with a freedom to investigate their sound without the pressure and judgment of performance attached to it. I knew I was onto something; it was just a matter of figuring out the best way to deliver it so that more people could experience the benefits.

Thanks to my work with Jeanie, I had a method for teaching vocal technique to students that was clear, effective, and kind. The Alexander Technique offered a process for helping individuals build an inner stillness and calm to their nervous systems. I had experienced this many times in my training course with Ann Rodiger. This process simultaneously supported one's music skills and amplified their stage presence.

But, as for expressing themselves without getting in their own way? In order to access that inner "goofy," or unfiltered, state, I found students needed to add one ingredient—movement. Both guided and intuitive movement helped students to keep their minds from constant self-judgment. Movement allowed singers to connect to their emotions without pretense, and without performing. Movement allowed them to get out of their heads.

Eventually, I began to see that I had a unique approach to teaching that made me stand apart from other voice teachers. Many teachers know an incredible amount of repertoire; some teachers are amazing accompanists; others are imbued with a deep knowledge of jazz history; some teachers emit gospel and R&B like it's coming out of their pores; numerous voice teachers have every muscle, ligament and bone memorized; and others are masterful guides at teaching improvisation.

I had this strange ability to help people sing in ways that felt easy and playful, yet powerful. Becoming embodied meant helping students connect to their bodies and not bypassing their feelings, but rather, using their emotions. I could teach students how singing worked and bring them inside the creative pulse of music and artmaking. Finally, I could nurture willing students to find their artistic passions while also helping them connect to the most fundamental part of performing—themselves.

SHAPES IN THE DARK

Intro:
D/A   Dbm
No light to distract me
          F
From your touch
D   Dbm
No thoughts just unwrap me
Ab sus2
I feel so much
D   Dbm
Let's escape with a cloud
F
I need someone I can trust

Chorus:
Gbm
Shapes in the dark
    Bm
Feel different
Gbm
Shapes in the dark
    Bm
Feel different

Verse:
D/A   Dbm
No light to distract me
              F
From your touch
D   Dbm
No thoughts just unwrap me
Absus2 (Ab)
I feel so much
D   Dbm
Let's escape with a cloud
F
I need someone I can trust

Interlude:

Chorus:

Verse 2:
D/A   Dbm
A chance to rest my eyes,
F
To smell
D/A   Dbm
And my skin is alive
Absus2 (Ab)
I can tell
D   Dbm
All the sounds underneath
F
Ring thru each cell

Bridge:

Ebm Bb   A
If I close my eyes
Ebm   Bbm A
Suddenly everything changes
Ebm   Bbm   A
There's a gift of surprise in the dark

Chorus:

Outro:

No light
No light
No light
No light…
It's sacred
No light
In the dark
No light
Turn on
No light
It's sacred
No light
In the dark
(Fade out)

Your Artistic Voice

Claiming

Trusting The Unknown

VOICE LOG #14

At some point, some part of your wild has got to be let out onstage. It may be a small stirring wild, it may be a groaning, or even a full out holler or belting wild. But at some point, your performing, your singing, even your audience is going to demand it.

JUST MUSIC

What is this language? music
That suddenly knows how to capture all the curves and edges of my
feelings,
of this moment

My biggest joy,
my deepest pain,
my burning anger,

My tears, my turn on and more

My wit,
my stream of consciousness,
run-on sentences,
And and and
this landscape,
this silence,

The fear in my belly,
my satisfaction...with just you.
Just music.
No words.

BUFFALO STANCE

"Lookin' good's a state of mind.[12]"

—NENEH CHERRY

I think every teenager feels like they're a rebel with a cause. And for a kid growing up in New York City, this is especially true. We were accustomed to the hustle and hustling, the homeless, the mohawked, the pierced, and piercing looks. We spent our time congregating in parks—like Washington Square or Sheep Meadow (aka "the Meadow") at Central Park, amongst weed dealers, squatters, and skateboarders—where kids would go to flirt, hook up, and share their spoils of weed, acid, and ecstasy, like it was gold. We traversed the city while gathering the strength needed to withstand the uncertainty and doubting voices in our own heads from music, clothing, and one another..

In middle school, my friends and I often split our time between the East Village and the Upper West Side of the city. We lived off the foods and mind-altering substances that those neighborhoods provided. From burritos, to falafel, to bagels with cream cheese and tomato. We absorbed the cultures and cuisines of Ukraine, China, Italy, and others as we strutted along the avenue adorned in sunglasses, hats, and earrings that we purchased from the stands lining St. Marks. We were developing our legs—legs that would help us to move beyond high school and the familiarity of our neighborhoods.

---

12   Neneh Cherry. "Buffalo Stance." *Raw Like Sushi*. Virgin, 1989.

Of course, some of what we put our energy into was slightly insignificant. Entrusting one friend to buy weed from a fake storefront, using another friend's food stamps to get McDonald's, and then setting up camp at my house (or Amber's, Anya's, Bekah's, or Becca's—two Rebecca's!). The objective was always the same—to keep fueling our collective in whatever way we saw necessary.

One way of feeding our group was through housing. Kids, especially teenagers, need places to go, and so we rotated locations throughout our high school days. Each campsite had a different feel. My friend Rebekah lived in the Dakota, a large Gothic castle-like building set beside ordinary cement and brick apartment buildings along West 72nd Street. It looked like the setting for a Sherlock Holmes or Agatha Christie mystery.

Bekah was the daughter of the late filmmaker, Albert Maysels, of Maysles Films—most known for their documentaries *Grey Gardens* and *Gimme Shelter*. Later, he and his wife, Gillian Walker, Rebekah's mother, established what is now The Maysles Documentary Center in Harlem. Of course, growing up, I had no idea what Albert Maysels' work was, nor the scope of his influence. But now I can see that the people surrounding me were proof that distinct voices and perspectives were needed in art and the world at large. At the time, Albert Maysles was just the older guy who showed up at breakfast with us from time to time as we scoured the kitchen looking for bread, butter, and cereal.

Bekah's home and family were another example of how one could design a life in the arts instead of a traditional work path. For instance, I knew nothing about the history of the Dakota and its architect, Henry Janeway Hardenbergh, but what I did know was that it housed legendary figures, such as John Lennon and Yoko Ono. It was also where John Lennon was tragically shot in 1980. Even after John Lennon was killed, Yoko Ono continued to live there with their son, Sean Lennon.

Besides the building's celebrity-like status, the design of Bekah's apartment felt like an extension of the artsiness and quirkiness of its inhabitants. I never could remember which of the myriad pathways we took to get to her chamber, and we rarely left the same way we had entered. You may have arrived on the first or second floor, but then exited through a bookcase that was, in fact, a door to the various halls within the building. It was as if Hardenbergh had designed a physical metaphor for life, and the many ways one could play it.

This was all quite different from our friend Amber's apartments. Amber lived in two separate places—both in the East Village. Her world felt more like my own, in both location and community. Raised by two uncles—one, her biological uncle, Steve, worked as a registered nurse. The other, Don, was a former partner who ran a non-profit for LGBTQIA youth. Don regularly shared his one-bedroom apartment with teens and young adults who were struggling at home or looking to get out on their own two feet in an unwelcoming world.

I never knew the people intimately, but often I would find myself in line for the shower or searching through the refrigerator for leftovers, standing next to another Black woman with voluminous hair and flaming red nails, who had stayed the night before. Although they were only a few years older than us, we saw the challenges of their circumstances, and the conviction they had to continue living their truth.

Whether at Amber's or Bekah's house, mine or Anya's, we usually traveled in a group—bonded together like a cluster of hydrangea or bubblegum. Sharing t-shirts, jeans, lipstick, exchanging jackets and hats as we passed cigarettes from hand to hand—everything was for the group. We would pool our money to get take-out, loosies, and forties. Our cause was everyone's cause. Bras—communal; sweatshirts—communal; pants—communal; and, of course, we borrowed from the closets of our friends' parents, as well. It was up to each kid to assess the rules of their own home. Whether poor or wealthy, white or of color, money didn't stop our need to make our individual stamp on the world. We had an abundance of free time and bravado to take care of that. I discovered that my family's income couldn't hinder my popularity, nor my sexuality. I could wield power with lipstick, short shorts, and a cigarette between my lips.

But it wasn't just the clothes—music made me feel strong, too. And with our own Buffalo Stance, my crew of friends swore upon the gospel according to Stevie Wonder, Bob Marley, and Prince. For those of us who loved to go dancing, like my friends Anya and Becca Cohen, we would travel to see live bands, like The Brand New Heavies, allowing the music to fill our well until it overflowed. We ventured to downtown clubs, like Wetlands, where the bouncers would turn a blind eye to the age requirement. We could dance for hours at parties, like Soul Kitchen—dripping sweat as bartenders poured us tequila shots—the room spinning with the thrill of our hormones, older guys, and music.

We were trying to feel comfortable in our own skin. Looking for the ground underneath our feet to remind us of our importance. As we searched, we found that strength in fashion, music, and in our loyalty to each other. Whether we were borrowing each other's address, clothing, or war paint, the aim was simple—to see if we could uncover a version of ourselves, someone in the mirror who we wanted to be, and continue pursuing, just as the bands we were following in the inky, grimy nights of New York.

THE GUARDED GATE

Washington Heights, 6pm

A medium built Black woman in her fifties stands in white capri shorts, a t-shirt, and a baseball cap. She has a fold-up lawn chair in her hand and a large straw bag over her shoulder. She leans against a wide brick entryway.

GLORIA

I don't know,
I don't know what I was worrying about
Look at these children!
Look at these young girls
Worried they ain't got nuthin'
Adding eyelashes, adding hair
Stretching their faces on those phones
Those phones!
Pssst!
But they got a whoooooollllle lot of somethin'
In every direction

GLORIA says with sass outlining her breasts and waist

Up here
Here
Back there

See that gate
You see it?
You see there's all them plants
And bushes and a few thorns here and there
But that's only natural
See everyone thinks that the gate is locked
It's never been locked!
Everybody just expects it to be
You can walk right up and go on through
I've been sitting here because I got all this yarn here
That I forgot about
While I was busy worrying
This yarn was just growing
Piling up
Piling up
And finally one day
I said "Enough!" They keep telling me that I gotta do this and do that.
"Enough! I'm going over to that gate and I'm gonna find a way to pick
that damn lock and get outta here!"
So I spent a lot of time preparing, you know?
Cause I'm not one to go anywhere without packing first. I had to go
food shopping 'cause I figure I'm gonna be sitting over there a long
time sorting that lock out.
Pssst!
So I make myself a nice turkey sandwich you know with greens I got
from the farmer's market
And some avocado and fresh tomatoes from my one little tomato
plant,
Cook up some cornbread,
Pack some fresh berries, fill my water bottle and off I go.
I had to bring my chair too 'cause I can't just be standing there all day

This right hip hurts me sometimes

GLORIA finally lets out a sigh as if she's been holding it in for some time

But you know I get to that gate
Take all this time packing a lunch, made sure to bring some extra clothes.
In case it got cool and I was still out there the next day I brought a blanket and some socks
Chile! I didn't need none of that!
When I made it up to that gate
Do you know what I saw?
That gate was cracked
The iron was all rusted and bent out of shape
I couldn't believe it!
Right where I thought there was going to be a lock
The gate wasn't even closed!
It was still open
And I had to think back

GLORIA furrows her brow

"What made me think this gate was locked? Who told me that?" I stood up there and pondered it for a while, a long time but I couldn't remember one specific person, it was too many to name honestly.
This book, that teacher, this famous interview, that special speech by so and so
You gotta be careful what you let your eyes see and your ears hear sometimes
I don't know what I was always worrying about
Why did I take their word for it?
I get up to that gate and I see there is mooooore than enough room for

me! and you and her and Them!
And that's why I'm telling you
These girls, these young women, I don't know what they're worrying for
They already got everything they need.

Fade to black

A GOOD TIME IS ENOUGH

"If there's something I need I don't already have, I know I'll get it from a good friend.[13]"

—BY EMILY KING

"When you got a good friend,
That will stay right by your side,
Give 'em all your spare time,
Try to love and treat 'em right.[14]"

—ROBERT JOHNSON

2022 began with an unexpected, yet welcome bang—or rather, a low, subterranean call—when I was invited to perform in the premiere of Ash and Adam Fure's *The Force of Things: An Opera for Objects[15]*, at the Hopkins Center for the Arts in Dartmouth, MA. Despite the reverberations of the Omicron variant that was rippling across the US and the globe, Dartmouth College decided to give *The Force* another go. The first attempt had been before the start of the pandemic in 2020, so, near-

---

13   King, Emily. "Good Friend." *The Switch*. Making Music, 2015.
14   Johnson, Robert. "When You Got a Good Friend." *King of the Delta Blues Singers*. Columbia, 1969.
15   Fure, Ashley and Adam. *The Force of Things: An Opera for Objects*. Performance. Darmstadt: Darmstadt Summer Courses, 2016.

ly two years later, they were going to try again.

The call to be a part of this project had come at the 11th hour, surprising me while I was still in quarantine. I received a message from my friend, César Alvarez, asking if I would consider being involved. I was just starting to feel like Humpty Dumpty—put back together again, with visible cracks. COVID-19 had drained a lot of my energy and motivation to do anything, so it was interesting that I was being asked to participate in a full-length concert. But I knew the change of scenery and connecting with friends, new and old, would do my body and mind good.

When we spoke on the phone, César let me know of the rehearsal and performance schedule, and also asked if I would like to visit their class at Dartmouth, where they had recently become an assistant professor of music. This opportunity sounded like the best of both worlds since I would get to perform, as well as teach, and meet developing artists. It was good timing, as well, since work was going to be slow in the beginning of January. It was the end of December, and the performance was just several weeks away. After days of laying in my bed, watching documentaries, and using my bedroom as a treadmill, I couldn't fully imagine what it would mean to be onstage again. I had some reservations but decided to say yes. As it turned out, saying yes was the right answer.

Fortunately for me, I had experienced Ash's work several years prior when I had the opportunity to perform in their piece, *Filament*[16], with The Philharmonic at Lincoln Center. Ash had composed the work in collaboration with Constellation Chor, an experimental vocal collective lead and founded by Marisa Michelson. I joined Constellation Chor as a guest for the premiere. Studying the music and black, custom 3-D printed megaphones—which were specially designed for us to sing through—exposed me to the vocal language, textures, and intentional movement of Ash's work.

---

16   Fure, Ashley. *Filament*. Performance. New York: David Geffen Hall, 2018.

Fure's music often explores the small and intimate vocal expressions of our humanity. *The Force of Things* was directly related to humans and our impact on and dialogue with nature. Ash's brother, Adam, created an opening installation for the opera—which was stunning! The audience was invited to step into the space onstage at the opening of each performance. Off-white crinkled paper hung from above, creating cave-like formations. Hidden within the bodies of each shape were speakers emitting low rumblings, often too low to detect aurally, yet could be felt physically. Fans blew gently rattling the atmosphere, and at set times, each sculpture would beat and tremble as if it were alive with questions, begging to be answered or merely heard. This was the stage which Samita and I stepped onto before uttering our first sounds into the air.

Samita Sinha was the other vocalist/performer. With a background as a dancer, choreographer, researcher and teacher—she and I had many overlapping interests. We started rehearsing the music together so that we could relax into our parts and find ourselves in the score. Although there wasn't a ton of music to learn, there was a deep and nuanced world to map out and understand. By the time opening night arrived, we had developed a sisterhood that tethered us to each other as we moved and vocalized throughout the performance.

Each day our small cast would learn a new piece of the puzzle. Some of the musicians had already been in *The Force of Things,* so they were accustomed to techniques for playing the instruments, as well as general directions. Every couple of days, a new element would be introduced—from various costuming, to lighting, to directing. After a week of rehearsing, we had a solid grasp of the material. The hive mind effect of people focused on a common goal had proven highly successful. Everything—from COVID-19 protocol, to our in-ear cues, learning to play massive monochords (a large stringed instrument that reverberated like whales communicating through time), to our collective vocal solos sung through talk boxes—created an otherworldly experience. Both on and offstage, through sound and silence, we were finding connections and creating a collective voice.

The day before dress rehearsal, we had a scheduled day off in which I was able to visit César's class. The class was held via Zoom in order to protect performers, crew, and students—but that didn't lessen my excitement. I couldn't wait to hear what the students were learning and writing about. I was also looking forward to the intimate cocoon that discussions amongst songwriters and artists often creates—the deep whys and hows that constantly pull at most artists. It had been years since I had had the pleasure to break bread with César, and I always love their creative work and conversation.

The last time I had worked directly with César had been for the elaborate dance theater piece *Full Still Hungry*[17], for which they composed the music. *Full Still Hungry* is an evening length concert investigating the hard-to-digest truths of food injustice and its impact on our lives. The performance was choreographed by my lovely friend, Ana Maria Alvarez (César's sister), and performed by the activist dance theater company Contra Tiempo, of which Ana is the founder. At the time César and I were lead singers with the live band that played for Contra Tiempo. Together we had taken on a range of voices and characters—from food justice storyteller, to Carmen Miranda, from pop rock fortune teller, to Salsero.

But that had been nearly 10 years ago. Since then, César had two more children, wrote their 5th musical entitled *Futurity*[18] (which won the Lortel Award for Outstanding Musical), co-founded Polyphone (a festival for new and emerging musicals at the University of the Arts in Philadelphia), and most recently, won a Guggenheim Fellowship. The thing that I love about César's music (and there are many things to love) is that they started as a singer/songwriter in a band touring throughout the States. They started like most performers, simply wanting to express the feelings they had inside. Eventually they decided their storytelling just needed a

---

17   Alvarez, Ana María, and César. *Full Still Hungry*. Contra Tiempo et al. Performance New York, NY, 2011.

18   Alvarez, César. "Futurity." *Futurity*. (New York: Theatre Communications Group, 2017.)

bigger platform, and that's how they began writing musicals.

The class that César invited me to was called Songwriting 2. The students who joined that day were a mix of instrumentalists, producers, songwriters, composers, and first-timers. Some were most comfortable performing music by other composers, while others were more accustomed to writing original music. Some students were digital music arts majors while others were performance majors in classical music. Some people made beats and others made instruments, yet all of them were looking for an authentic connection and expression through music.

Before getting into our deeper music and life dilemmas, as songwriters love to do, César first asked me to introduce myself to the group. I told the facts that many people surmise when they hear my last name—that my father is a composer and multi-instrumentalist, that my mother is a dancer/choreographer (now manual and movement therapist), and that I grew up in a vibrant world of performing artists. As a child, I danced in modern dances choreographed by my mom, sang and wrote music with a band in middle school and high school, performed back-ups for friends' bands, and traipsed around New York City to every kind of show imaginable. Still, the lingering questions, "Why do you sing? Why is making music important to you?" hung in cyberspace.

For some reason, the closest and most instinctual thing can often be the hardest to identify. In the last five to ten years, I've realized that creating evocative and impressive works of art isn't my sole purpose for composing. Yes, I want to captivate audiences and draw them into rich sound journeys that will hopefully change or transform them for the better. That would be nice—to know that the hours of singing, playing piano, writing in notebooks, and rehearsing were worth it. But there's another reason. As much as I love being onstage and recording albums, I also love the thing that my friend and guitarist, John Caban, used to call "the hang." It is perhaps the thing that touches me equally, if not more than performing itself. Sometimes the real reason I make music is to spend time doing this incredibly magical thing with friends who also love and enjoy doing this incredibly magical thing. It seems so obvious, but I have to admit that a part of me forgot. After so much time working to improve my vocal technique and songwriting voice, it didn't occur to me that it was equal doses of music and friendship that made the secret sauce.

As I got older and began a family, and others began families, as well—moving to different parts of the world and taking on bigger jobs and responsibilities made it increasingly difficult to just play. During high school and college, spending time with friends was a given, but it became more challenging between bedtimes, mealtimes, after school activities, and sheer exhaustion. When I said this, César lit up, echoing my sentiment. They, too, had recently realized that throwing parties was a key component of their artistic process for the same reason.

"The hang" is a spiritual technology, a return to ourselves and our human instinct for collaboration. It's why mentorship and apprenticeship mean so much to one's development in the arts. I experienced this very clearly several years ago when I was invited to teach at Jazz Camp West—a music and dance camp for arts lovers of all ages. The motto for their organization is "transforming lives through music," and after a week of making music, eating, dancing, performing, teaching and learning from others in the Redwoods of La Honda, California, that's when it really hit me. That's what I'm trying to do—transform a life through music. My own and others'. And so often it begins with the connection of two people just having a good time.

VOICE LOG #88

...The question is how do I let go?

INTERGALACTIC INTERLUDE

I'm looking for a song
Looking for a song
Looking for a song

                                                Follow me

I'm looking for a song
Looking for a song
Looking for a song

                                      (Come,) bend your knee
                                            Bend-n-breathe

I'm looking for a star
Looking for a road
That'll take me far
Far away

                                            Bend your knee
                                          Bend-n-breathe

                                            Step close
                                    Smell the seed
                                        Jump up
                                    Tap your feet
                                        Step close
                                      Just believe
                                        Step close
                                  Follow your feet

I'm looking for a song
Looking for a song

Looking for a song
I heard that song
I remember

                                                    Follow me

I'm looking for a song
Looking for a song
Looking for a song
I remember

                                                    Follow me

I heard that song!
I'm looking for a song
Looking for a song
Looking for
I remember

                                                    Follow me

An it right here
Right here
An it right here
Right here!
An it right here
I remember
Looking for a song
Looking for a song...

WRITING ON A WIRE

I'm walking on a tightrope
The edge of a sidewalk
Balancing
One foot in front of the other
Step by step
My arms are the wings to my airplane
Light as parchment
Focused as feathers
Aiming my beak towards a dream
I imagined
While awake
Looking down
Looking ahead
Drifting
My will solid as cement
still
I could fall
Dive
Fly
And no one would even know
No one would ever know
I could evaporate
or
sink into
Distilled dimensions
of Joy or sadness

Either way
Drowning in ecstasy
I could be anywhere and here all at once
Balancing on a tightrope
Walking on the edge of a sidewalk
Looking over a cliff
Deciding whether or not to fly

Vocal Identity

VOICE LOG #21

I always knew I was Black, skinny, and a girl—but I never knew what my voice would be.

FIREFLY

"Firefly: A soft-bodied beetle related to the glowworm, the winged male and flightless female of which both have luminescent organs. The light is chiefly produced as a signal between the sexes, especially in flashes.[19]"

It was a Tuesday morning in the middle of February, which is partly why it surprised her so that, upon waking, she found herself slightly iridescent. Dreary from so many dark, winter nights accumulating like the piles of snow on the perimeters of the sidewalk, she could feel the accumulation of long days of teaching, and longer nights begging for answers of her own, adding up. Yet without her awareness, a light began to shine inside her. Strange light. Not quite blue, not quite yellow, not quite silver or gold. Somewhere between all four, she started to glow—just subtly enough that most people, average people, wouldn't notice. It started with her hair. Black to begin with, it had taken on an extra shine, even though she hadn't washed it in over a week, and in certain light, it appeared as though glitter had been shaken over her head. Her toenails and fingernails didn't need any polishing because they, too, were shining. But big changes often start in subtle ways. They creep in slowly.

Every day she had been feeling just a little bit lighter, despite the heaviness of winter. And every day she would find some strange gray-

19   Encyclopedia.com. N.d. "Firefly." Accessed May 23, 2023. https://www.encyclopedia.com/plants-and-animals/animals/zoology-invertebrates/firefly

veined piece of eggshell, or what seemed like plaster, in odd places throughout her apartment. On the countertop, or the bathroom sink, or on her pillow when she woke up in the morning. She usually wrote it off as another one of the side effects of having old landlords and a rent-stabilized apartment.

But that one Tuesday morning in the middle of February, she felt something was different with herself. Every mirror that she passed seemed to be reflecting her image with a flickering candlelight—like an old photograph, but in real time. That magic puff of camera dust that you see in movies. But it was nearly 7:55 AM and she didn't have time to start looking through her books on goddesses or tarot decks for answers. Instead, she grabbed her purse, phone, plastic container of whatever leftovers she had placed in the fridge the night before, along with the golden milk that she was trying in an attempt to eliminate her coffee habit, and left for work.

Sitting on the subway, she began to regret not driving. Her hour-glass figure perfectly sandwiched between a man with a protruding beer belly on her right, and a pregnant woman on her left. Although she physically fit in her seat, something inside her felt bigger than the space she was occupying. Her body cast a slight yellow light. "Is it happening again? Wait, this is getting crazy," she thought to herself. Ever since she had returned to singing, strange things had started happening.

Each day it was as if old parts of her were falling off, like chipped paint. The first week of singing, when she came home to take a bath, she had noticed that she barely needed to turn on the hot water. Her body was already warm. When she stepped onto her bathmat afterwards, staring at her naked brown body in the mirror, she noticed a new suc-culence—like what she imagined people always said about pregnant women. Rather than rushing to put on her cocoa butter, she admired her legs, arms and buttocks, more pleased than usual—thinking that perhaps those 15-minute online workouts were having an effect.

She had only begun taking singing lessons as a dare. Her friend, Mona, had challenged her to sing Whitney Houston's "How Will I

Know[20]" at a karaoke bar. Either the sake or the martinis had been so strong that night, and their bellies so empty, that her whole group of friends inspired the entire place to start chanting her name—"LaTasha! LaTasha! LaTasha!"

"You're a natural girl! You have got to start taking voice lessons," Mona said, while searching aimlessly through her purse.

"Why?" she answered, almost annoyed. "So I can join *The Voice*?" she asked as she rolled her eyes.

"You never know," her friend Matteo added, leaning like the Tower of Pisa from so many cocktails.

"For real, you LOVE singing—why don't you just try it?" Mona said, her fingers stopping on a pack of gum that clearly had been living at the bottom of her bag for some time.

"Why would I even do it now? It's not like I'm going to perform anywhere or make an album!" Even as she said the words, she felt her heart betray her, quickening its pace. She had always wanted to record an album of her own music.

At home, in her powder blue nightstand, like a secret treasure chest, she had stored pages and pages of notebooks with lyrics. Melodies which she had poured into ink on page. Love songs, protest songs, songs to heal her students, songs to mend the worn away parts of her parents' marriage, and songs to heal herself. But she couldn't imagine sharing any of this with her friends right now. In their inebriated state, it was hard to trust their sincerity. Right then, Mona turned to her, placing LaTasha's hand inside her own as if she were about to propose. "I'm going to get you voice lessons." And that was it.

Two weeks later, LaTasha was standing in a small, 8x10 room with a woman she had never met, telling her about her dream to make an album. The teacher was roughly her height of around 5'5," but nearly double her width. With a full, glorious afro, she always greeted LaTasha with a wide smile, like the curtains on a stage being drawn to begin a

---

20   Whitney Houston. "How Will I Know." *Whitney Houston. Arista,*
      1985.

concert. Tami was her name. She was incredibly encouraging and treat-
ed each of LaTasha's wishes like they could be a reality, but LaTasha still
felt like a fake when the words leapt out of her mouth. "I want to make
an album."

She had never worked with a band. The only performance experience she had was helping backstage with theater productions during
college and singing with her school's a cappella group, The Harmoneers.
As much as she had felt like a fraud in that lesson, she left feeling different. A kind of zing had started. Something in her belly was buzzing and
ever since, she couldn't bring herself to stop. It was almost a year later
and LaTasha was still taking voice lessons.

"So, what are you working on these days? When are you going to
sing for us?" her friend Jasmine asked flirtatiously.

"I don't have anything to sing. We just do warmups," she said—
which was true, but also a bit of a lie. LaTasha had been learning a jazz
standard called "Bye Bye Blackbird," and had also begun putting her lyrics to music with the help of her teacher. She had also found a guitarist
for the first time in her life. The thought of it made her so nervous and
excited that it made her have to pee. She excused herself from the table.

Walking through the darkly-lit Mexican restaurant, Mi Corazon,
their weekly meetup spot, she found the restroom and quickly closed
the door behind her. Unbuttoning her stretch jeans, she watched as her
stomach breathed a sigh of relief, exhaling as she released her trepida-
tion. She wiped herself, like a mother caring for her baby, and pulled up
the new lace underwear she had bought to celebrate her bravery. She
always did something for herself to celebrate newfound courage, but
since her friends knew about this tradition, she chose something they
wouldn't see. She stepped out of the stall and into the washroom when
she saw it again—that strange, beaming reflection. It teased her, appear-
ing as a gold statue.

It was undeniable, and yet the women around her didn't seem to
notice at first. But then, another young Black woman with locs walked
past LaTasha, her mouth agape, and casually said, "Nice glow, sis!"

"Huh?" LaTasha stuttered and closed her mouth as the woman began sudsing her hands rhythmically. LaTasha was about to reapply her lip gloss when she realized that she didn't need to—her lips were already shimmering that same iridescent hue. Strange light. Not quite blue. The same hue she thought she had seen in the mirror earlier that day. Bouncing off her shoulders and stomach as if crushed crystals had been gently blown into the air around her. She started to suspect that she was hallucinating, but when this complete stranger commented on her glow, it made her wonder if something was, in fact, different.

"Your skin...it's like you're, I don't know...glowing," the woman said casually, but surprised. "I mean, you look great! Whatever you're doing, keep at it, because it is working! Black girl magic, right?" the woman said, winking. She walked out while drying her hands on a paper towel.

LaTasha started to feel her heart beating faster and faster. She was certain she could hear it vibrating off the bathroom walls. She felt as if she might levitate, that this was related to the new drink she had ordered—winged woman. Something was not right, and yet, when she thought about it, everything had been different since she started singing again.

All she had done was say yes to a dare. A dare to do something that she had balled up inside layers and layers for years. Something that—when the right amount of soup and sushi had been consumed—had made her forget her purposeful and practical ways, causing her to serenade her friends as if her soul's existence depended on it. That night at karaoke, she had forgotten her friends were watching, forgotten how her hair looked, and forgotten that she was up way past her bedtime. Something in her let go, in the way that skydivers or bungee jumpers look falling backwards into the air, trusting and reveling in being alive at the same time. She had finally given herself over to something she had wanted, the same way she wanted that guy who worked at the bar next door to her house.

Come to think of it, every time she saw him, it seemed that he too would flash an orange glow underneath the rust and maroon-colored t-shirts he wore. Those half-faded t-shirts, slightly clinging to his chiseled waist and arms, which she admired every time he bent down to get ice. Like the woman in her yoga class who rippled with light through her torso, as if her actual organs were glowing, any time she talked about salsa dancing.

Just as she made the connection, LaTasha felt her face start flickering. Strange light. Not quite blue, not quite yellow, not quite silver or gold. This time she was sure of what she was seeing, but there was no one with her in the bathroom to witness it. The crescendo and decrescendo of light—swelling and dimming and swelling again—as she stared at her lone portrait in the mirror. Just like a firefly—except she was standing in a small, dimly lit public bathroom in a Mexican restaurant in the middle of Brooklyn. But big changes often start in subtle ways. They creep in slowly.

MISSING VOCAL IDENTITY

"Free your mind and the rest will follow.[21]"

—En Vogue

Over the years, I've had many students comment on their own voices saying things like, "Ugh, I sound squeaky," "It just sounds thin," or, longingly, "I really want to be able to sing low." Everyone is so quick to judge themselves. What has become both comical and slightly sad is how early in a lesson students will start to dissect themselves. I often have to reassure them, "You know, we've only done one exercise so far and this *is* practice time," to which they usually smile, seeing the irony. Students often come to me with a variety of wishes ranging from wanting to sing higher, to belt, to stop straining, or just wanting to feel comfortable with their voices.

Somewhere deep inside, under years of pushing those wishes to the back of the line (or their throats), they arrive at my studio ready to face their desires and their fears. They come with dreams to learn a song, record an album, integrate voicework into their performance practice, accompany themselves singing, or sing for a special event. Even though there may be a specific thing coming in the future, most of them have wanted this for a long time. But it's difficult to realize when *their* specific voice, and not the sound of their favorite singer, comes out of their mouth. When it's actually their voice bouncing off the walls and return-

---

21   En Vogue. "Free Your Mind." *Funky Divas.* Eastwest, 1992.

ing to them, it can sometimes be like vocal dysmorphia. Like putting on new glasses and having to adjust one's perspective.

After I graduated college and completed my teacher certification in the Alexander Technique, and then Somatic Voicework™, the LoVetri Method, and after I cut my teeth teaching at Brooklyn Conservatory (I am still grateful to Earl McIntyre for giving me a starting teaching position), I decided to officially grow my own boutique voice studio. Teaching at the conservatory had its own kind of learning curve. I had to adapt and work with students of every age, learning ability, and learning style, as well as build a catalog of easy yet effective vocal exercises (which I thankfully found through Somatic Voicework™), find repertoire, as well as prepare students for and put on recitals. It was a bit intimidating and sometimes terrifying. But over the years, I got the hang of it and started to learn where my teaching strengths lie. It was from there that I grew confident enough to open my own private studio at home.

Gradually, I built my little studio where I could teach voice and Alexander Technique. Alexander Technique was something that I wove into singing lessons. It was like the stock for my stew or the backdrop over which I laid Somatic Voicework™. Alexander Technique gave me the ability to see students' movements, where their tension was originating from, and how it might be contributing to specific areas like their neck, jaw, or tongue. I could hear when someone wasn't breathing or when there was constriction on the back left side of their throat. Somatic Voicework™ helped me to develop this kind of listening. But it went further—I went from sensing muscular tension to sensing people's emotional and energetic energy. I'm sure the same thing must happen for counselors and therapists. Once I was in a position to listen to others day after day, my sensitivity heightened to observing how students felt about themselves and their voices.

Despite what they said they wanted from our first meeting, many students felt uncomfortable being loud, opening their mouths, or felt embarrassed singing in front of another person. One person might want to be noticed, but then get defensive when I offered suggestions for how to make that possible. Some people needed to feel a sense of control, while others wanted to finally loosen their grip on music and life in general. I listened and offered exercises, artists to study, and songs that would best support the individual needs of each student.

In the beginning, most of my adult students were singer/songwriters. They were passionate and didn't need convincing that music was powerful or exciting. It was easy for them to feel the connection to the music that they practiced. Usually, these students struggled more with vocal technique, which interfered with their ability to fully express themselves creatively. Their artistic motivation gave them a sense of musical purpose and fulfillment

For years I saw a woman named Eva. Eva was of medium height and build and had brown hair. She had been performing with an alternative band and writing originals, so she already had a solid base of musical understanding. In college, Eva majored in jazz piano, but more recently had started playing electric bass and, of course, singing. She was kind and thoughtful. One unique thing about Eva was that, in addition to her musical knowledge, it was quite easy for her to connect to her body, especially when I gave her specific cues. Cues that helped her focus on softening the back of her tongue and throat were particularly helpful. One of Eva's main goals as a singer was to be able to sing with power and belt. She wanted to be able to sing with her full voice and heart, without wavering or holding back. Eva knew that in order to get there, she couldn't simply copy incredible singers, like Aretha Franklin. She had to find her own power in singing. Therefore, as with much skill-building, that meant a lot of "two steps forward, one step back" in order to progress.

Eva and I worked together for years. As I grew as a teacher, she also grew as a singer. Part of that growth for Eva arrived in the form of owning what she wanted. When she initially came to me, she wanted, like many students, to sing better, to iron out vocal parts, and to "not sound bad." But as her vocal strength grew, so did her confidence and along with it, her goals. I worked on helping Eva to build more volume in her singing voice without straining and feeling comfortable. However, being comfortable didn't mean that she wouldn't have to up the ante.

To increase her vocal strength, Eva had to gradually increase her breath support and stamina. Since she was committed to her home practice, there were many days that Eva was able to belt. The trouble was that she could only maintain it in my studio. Even though she knew the warmups and had plenty of lessons to practice with at home, she couldn't fully access her vocal power when she was alone. When she was at home, that kind of power felt unfamiliar and she kept reverting to singing quietly.

Then one day Eva shared with me, "You know, I'm the quiet one in my family. I never stand out or push my opinion. That's my sister." This was one of the earlier instances when I experienced a student making connections between their personal life, identity, habits, and their singing. It was a huge "A-Ha!" The role Eva played in her family conflicted with her new desire to stand out as a singer. I wouldn't have known this or made the connection had Eva not been willing to go inward, reflect on herself, and voice it to me. That's when I realized just how valuable student insights were to their own musical progress.

Eva had to want to change her own role, or identity as the "quiet one," to fully elevate her singing. She had to give herself permission to be loud—both vocally and in other parts of her life. This also explained what I felt on an intuitive level—that there were often deeper reasons as to why it took time for students to free their voices, in spite of having all the technical abilities to do so. They had to shift their mindset as well.

Another student started coming to me as a hobbyist. Francine was retired, a bit shy, yet super consistent and lovely to work with. She had been married for many years, loved gardening, and wanted to sing for pleasure. From her first lessons, Francine trusted me and opened up to me as a student. I felt honored, knowing how bashful she was. After a year or so of regular practice, she developed strong singing skills—more so than many of my other students because of how diligent she was with in-person lessons and home practice. For a while, we worked on releasing her voice to build her head register. It took many months to expose Francine to the range of sounds that she was capable of making. I began telling students during their introductory lessons that we were going for a "vocal tour" in order to help them adjust their mindset to the full range of sounds their voices could make.

Francine had been developing her head register and it was now something she was comfortable hearing. She could sing high, on different vowels, loudly and softly. At times she needed a little encouragement, but the notes were there. She learned to apply this to different songs she liked to sing. We eventually started working on her lower register. As much as singing in a high voice had made her feel like shutting her ears, working to develop her chest register was a different challenge altogether. Even though it was accessible and didn't cause her any pain, when Francine made sounds in her chest register, she didn't like it.

Sometimes she would giggle with discomfort. Hearing her voice in that way felt foreign. She often commented, "I sound like a man," after which she would laugh and jokingly imitate herself. Again, I was witnessing a student hearing their voice in an unexpected way and observing their struggle to integrate a new part of themselves. Neither Eva nor Francine were particularly resistant to exploring new aspects of their voices, but at the same time, they were uncomfortable with these new vocal identities that were revealing themselves.

Even when people want to change things about their singing or speech, they often have vocal characteristics that they're also reluctant to let go of. When I was studying with Jeanie, it took me a while to get used to the sound of my head register. People identify themselves with a certain pitch range, volume, or timbre, and to divert from that feels as if they are changing a part of who they are. Fortunately, people—just like sound—are pliable.

Improvisation and play in general can be tremendously effective in helping students achieve their music goals. When I invite singers to explore sound with a spirit of play, they often release set definitions about themselves giving their voices free range. I've watched students' faces glow with delight as they witness their own metamorphosis. It takes time to embrace and embody those changes, yet in every instance where a student gives themself permission to be more than they expected, I find myself in awe of human potential.

SHEDDING SKIN

(A blues)

Feels like shedding skin
Feels like
Feels like shedding skin
Feels like
Feels like shedding skin
Don't know where I start nor where I'll end

Feels like shaky ground
Under my feet
Feels like shaky ground
Under my feet
Feels like shaky ground
Hope my legs are strong enough to carry me

I been shapeshifting
I been
I been shapeshifting
I been
I been shapeshifting
Since the very very beginning

HEAD FULL OF HAIR

"Say it loud, I'm Black and I'm proud![22]*"*

—JAMES BROWN

When I was growing up there were two things I wasn't allowed to have—pork, and a perm. Two things that didn't matter much around white people, but *definitely* made me stand out around Black folks. In the 80s, when Jheri curls, relaxers and perms were everywhere, and bacon always smelled good—both were off limits. These were strict orders from my parents—my artist parents, who gave me a lot of free rein. I started flying by myself at the age of five, my curfew in middle and high school was quite malleable (so long as my parents knew who I was hanging out with), and the only fashion statement my dad really disapproved of was wearing all black.

They encouraged me to discover the world and receive it with all my senses. Many of the things that I was given access to were free-spirited, like the music and dance that they raised me around. There were no rules around religion. We didn't go to church, but my parents also didn't object to church. They weren't particular about the race, gender, sexuality, religion, nor the social class of my friends. Yet, while my friends were testing boundaries, shoplifting, or stealing credit cards, I was watching from the sidelines. But bacon and a perm—those were

---

22   Brown, James. "Say It Loud—I'm Black and I'm Proud." *A Soulful Christmas.* King, 1968.

two things I yearned for.

You wouldn't know from seeing pictures of me as a newborn—a little baby with straight, black hair and pale skin—that that baby would turn into a child with a mountain of hair on her head. I weighed 5 pounds, 6 ounces at full-term, and, like my own daughter, I took a few months to really gain my rolls and dimples. As I got older, just like my growing physical mass, my hair grew in volume too. By the age of five, I had enough hair to gather into bundles for two unapologetic afro puffs.

I used to go to beauty shops, or my aunt's or grandmother's chair, and have my hair done—pressed and shined to go to church, or the Kingdom Hall, or just so that my relatives had a way to keep it under control. Back then, people didn't use blow dryers to straighten hair—it was the hot comb, and only the hot comb. Before my hair could be pressed and curled, I would often feel the anticipation and concern of the hairdresser. Most people, encountering my hair for the first time, would exclaim, "Girl, you got a head full of hair!" They would try to make it sound like an observation, but I knew they were thinking, "Lawd, this chile's hair is going to take me foreva!" It did mean a lot of combing, brushing, parting, stretching, combing again, parting, oiling, pulling, and brushing for them. It meant that my hair wouldn't be done quickly, which meant that I was a time-intensive client, and therefore *I* wasn't easy. My hair was going to have a say in how things went. It wouldn't just be pushed around by some comb or brush without asserting itself. Unlike my well-behaved manners, my hair would resist, hold onto its opinion, push back, and loudly insist.

Naturally, with a head full of hair, I was also tender-headed—not unlike my personality. While I liked meeting people and going to new places, tasting and trying new things, I was also stubborn and secretly shy, easily defensive, and quite sensitive. Not only did it take a long time to comb through my hair, but, as the beauticians would see it, I also had the nerve to whine about it. I tried not to complain or be a burden, but it was hard to sit there without a whimper as my hair was being yanked and singed. "Girl, you tender-headed?" a family member or hairdresser would ask incredulously. I never understood the irritation in their voice, frustrated that I might make a fuss. To them, *they* were doing all the work. I'll add that this was before the days of detangler, leave-in conditioner, and other hair treatments. (Young people, please be grateful—life has never been as good as it currently is for natural Black hair. When I was growing up, it was just hair oil and deal with it.)

As strong as my hair was, water was the only element more powerful than my tresses. The rain, a pool, a beach, or any other body of water was undefeated when it came to my hair. Even sweating and playing outside, throwing firecrackers on a hot July evening could be redeemed, but Black hair has never been water-resistant. Occasionally a beautician would try to act on my behalf, like when I would visit my Aunt Sheila, my mother's youngest sister. She worked at a hair salon in Columbus, Georgia, and sometimes she would bring me with her. At some point, the unavoidable question ("You sure you don't wanna get a perm?") would arise. In my mind, I would respond, "Yes! Yes! I do! I'll take one. You can give me a perm!" But my Auntie or Grandmother would interject to tell them that I was not allowed.

As for the pork permission slip—I didn't start eating pork until a few years ago, and still only eat it occasionally. I fault my Austrian American husband. Pork is practically the national meat in Austria. My father-in-law loves pork so much he used to smuggle rolls of salami and speck, a smoked ham with large amounts of fat in it, into the States when returning from a visit home. So, were it not for my husband, I'm pretty sure I wouldn't eat pork—it rarely satisfies my cravings the way that beef does. But that crispy, salty, crackling flavor of bacon does entice me, from time to time.

Growing up, my father insisted that I not eat it. He never explained why, but I assume—like many other Black folks influenced by the Black Power movement, and Black Muslim thought of the 60s and 70s—it was because pigs were thought to be unclean animals. But this aspect of the Black identity movement only made me feel like more of an outsider amongst my extended family. There were many instances, in various kitchens, when I would be the exception.

If I was visiting my Uncle Paul (my mother's older brother, now deceased), for example, happily awaiting the breakfast his mother-in-law prepared, I would be rudely awakened from my pork daydream. I would be there with my cousin Patrice, my younger cousin Rhea (who we called Riri), and my older cousin, Eddie, (also now deceased) laughing and enjoying the morning. Their grandma would still be in her hair rollers and pink slippers, the smell of eggs sizzling, toast waiting to be draped in butter and jam, and a pile of bacon accumulating on oil soaked paper towels. I would often think, "This is it. This time I'm gonna get a piece!" But, just when I thought I could slip past their bacon radar, she would inevitably shout, "Pyeng can't have any bacon!" I would sulkingly take my plate and retreat.

Those two rules made me stick out like the pom-poms sprouting from my head. It felt like my parents had destined us for a life of not-your-average-Black-family. I lived in a city like no other, in a neighborhood where no one blinked if you had five-inch fingernails or wore rainbow dreadlocks to your ankles. I went to a predominantly white school where my parents would pick me up dressed in cowboy boots, hand painted skirts, and sunglasses from outer space. Christina and Henry didn't do discreet. They did loud, against the grain, out of the box, and into the future. But over time I realized that *they* weren't all that strange—no more than the world at large—and that bacon and perms would be just fine without me.

FINDING MY INNER BAD GIRL

For most of my life, I feel like I've been a "good girl"—an obedient daughter, an average student, and deeply interested in the world. I took on responsibility well and was independent from an early age. I made myself pleasing to others and amused adults and peers alike with my genuine enthusiasm, humor, and agreeable nature. But part of this was also due to my circumstance of being an only child and mostly raised by a single mother. From a young age, I knew how to lighten the mood and make others feel comfortable. I didn't realize it then, but I was always an empath. And, being an only child, I spent an abundance of time accommodating rules and behavior set by the adults. So I needed spaces to unleash myself. Clowning around and singing allowed me to release my inner people-pleaser and be unruly.

As much as I enjoyed disrupting things, I also did what my parents told me to do. If my mom said to use the money she had given me for eggs and olives, I used it for eggs and olives. If my dad said that I couldn't go on a school trip, then I didn't go. (Although, one time, in elementary school, I went swimming on a winter day after he specifically told me not to do so. My dad had been concerned about the cold making me sick, but I went anyway and suffered through the lecture.) If I did do something I wasn't supposed to do, I was generally pretty good at not getting caught. I was ever conscious of what was expected of me and knew when I was standing too close to the edge, so I just made sure I wasn't seen jumping off.

Being a Scorpio, I had an instinct for both camouflage and performance and preferred to lie rather than face confrontation. But don't get me wrong—I loved to talk too much, too loudly, and pass notes at the back of the class. My friends and I shared homework responsibilities like it was a small business. We worked at not working. We swapped textbooks, divided homework assignments, and coordinated test answers so as not to spend *all* our "precious time" studying. But it wasn't until my senior year in high school that I really decided to let loose.

The summer before my last year of high school, I was living in San Diego, CA with my mom, where I had recently acquired a stepfather. Being an east coast transplant, I felt like I had endured a six-month sentence in suburban hell. Living in the literal and figurative deserts of San Diego, without an escape plan or driver's license or close tribe, it became crystal clear to me that I absolutely did *not* want to live outside of New York City. Like many teenagers, I too was addicted to my surroundings. Although we claimed to be independent and hard, we often clung to the familiar like toddlers sucking on oversized pacifiers for safety.

My mother married at midnight on New Year's Eve, on a beach in San Diego. I remember the dress I wore—a sage-colored velvet, form-fitting mermaid skirt and a top that clung to me, just as I was clinging to my life in New York City. Six months later, at the end of the school year, with the permission of my mother, I packed my things and flew back home to New York, resettling into our Lower East Side studio of seventeen years. Thank goodness my mom had had the foresight to hold onto our place while we were gone!

She and my stepfather were following their love and working to blend two children from previous marriages, furniture, dishes, diets, and family traditions, but there wasn't much transition time. It was truly a case of bad timing for me. No teenager wants to change schools, especially in high school, unless they're asked to do so and given some say in the matter. The shock is too strong for pubescent hormones, causing your system to crash or explode—which mine nearly did.

I moved back to New York a few days after school ended. Two of my close friends, Kate and Ha-chi, moved into my old apartment with me, and I immediately started feeling like myself again. Kate and I had been friends since elementary school, and later traveled to India together.

She had always craved a little risk, coupled with her love of art and the outdoors. Dirty blonde, with green eyes and quite petite, she stood at about 5'6". Kate had grown up in Chelsea mostly with her single mother, Linda, a photographer and photo editor, and her older sister, Amy.

Ha-chi was the oldest of four girls, and the daughter of a Russian mother from Brooklyn, and a Chinese immigrant father. Like so many mothers, she knew how to weave a spell of possibility so that her daughters could create a future beyond what she had. Ha-chi and her sisters had grown up shuffling between homes until they arrived at an amazing squatter building on East 2nd Street where Tsana, her mother, remains to this day. That apartment, and Tsana's cooking, became a refuge for many of us throughout high school and early adulthood. From her mother, Ha-chi inherited a drive to work hard and nurture spaces, which she would take with her into each of her professions later in life.

The three of us managed to live together in that one-bedroom studio in the summer before my senior year. Our rent was just under $300 a month. There was only one official bedroom, at the front of the apartment, that looked out onto 6th Street. The room had a full-size pull-out futon, which two of us could sleep on together. The other sleep option was a loft bed built over the kitchen. In between the two sleeping sections of the apartment, there was a small dining area which often became a dance floor after hours. There was a round table and chairs, which sat across from a mini couch for guests. Overhead, my mother had hung a large mirror that covered the width of the wall and helped to create the illusion of more space.

That summer we reveled in attending drum circles in Prospect Park, eating plates of rice with peas and curry, drinking beverages like coconut water and sugar cane juice, meeting older guys, and smoking inordinate amounts of weed. We napped for 2-3 hours every day, our bodies desperate to recharge, exhausted from our malnourished teenage diets. It was a far cry from life in San Diego, for which I was utterly grateful. Kate was in her long flowing hair, skirts, unshaven armpits, and baking bread phase. I was in my lapa wraps, smoking cigarettes, and dreadlocks phase. And Ha-chi? Ha-chi was busy professionally dancing with the Feld Ballet. Although she was goofy and always ready for a joint, a joke or a drink, Ha-chi's inner bad girl had set hours—unlike the rest of us. After her freshman year, she dropped out of high school (later receiving her GED) to become a full-time dancer. From 9 AM to 5 PM, Ha-chi was occupied—stretching her body, mind, and strength to the edge.

For a few months, we played *Three's Company*. We cooked, laughed, danced, listened to records on my mom's record player, and met several inconsequential guys. We flirted with fire but didn't burn. After a few months, it became clear that our apartment was just *too close for comfort,* so Kate moved back home to her mom's loft to continue her year off before college.

For me, on the other hand, school was just about to begin and with it came new temptations to break the rules. The school I went to, Friends Seminary, was a private, Quaker school, which I had been attending since the age of three. I had grown up nestled in a community of staff and faculty who all knew and supported me. It was wonderfully safe, and at times almost too familiar, easy to take advantage of. And yet within all that was familiar, there was also a lack of *my* familiar. I couldn't find my history in it. That lack of seeing myself made me restless and angry inside. Although I had so many people around me who were supportive, I also felt alone.

It must have started pretty innocently at first, but as time crept on, it sunk into my head that I was the only one setting the rules. Before my senior year, I had never really given my inner Jekyll a chance to fully come out of hiding. For once I decided not to care about what others told me to do as much as I cared about what *I wanted to do.*

My dad lived a short journey of only four blocks away, on East 10th Street, but I didn't see much of him. After returning from San Diego, neither he nor my mother had insisted that I live with him, or any adult. Mainly I was mainly responsible for myself, but with the financial support from my mom, who would send me money for part of the rent and expenses each month. The rest of the bills—like the phone and electric bills—I paid by working odd end jobs babysitting, or working part time scooping ice cream at Ben & Jerry's, or assisting our super, Kadet, with selling her handmade leather goods at a flea market in Soho.

At other unexpected times I would see my fairy godmother, Laurie Carlos (aka "Aunt Laurie"), who at the end of our meal would slip me a $100 bill, knowing I was in need of it. It was a bit of a discombobulated system, but what could you expect from a seventeen-year-old? I still had it together just enough to make it through each month fed, clothed, and somehow passing my classes. I also had a circle of people to help me as I sailed through the patchy waters of senior year.

Most of my days went something like this: wake up at 12 PM or 1pm, wash my face, brush my teeth, adjust my hair or just put on a hat, throw a jacket over my pajamas, put on some shoes, and walk to school. On the days I attended it would often be to the shock and surprise of many of my friends, like Amber, who would exclaim, "Oh, you're here?!" I would *endure* the last period of English, or whatever subject I made it in time for, before convening with friends in Stuyvesant Park to smoke cigarettes, roll a blunt, and grab some junk food from the corner store. Then I would head back home to start the real "beginning" of my day. Several friends, like my friend Rachel, Melissa, and Ronah, would often join me or meet at my place later.

By the time Ha-chi arrived home from work, there would often be a small gathering of friends in our apartment. We would have smoked again and been working on a plan for making food. After eating and smoking more cigarettes, eventually friends would peel off leaving myself, and Ha-chi, and often our friend Miriam—who lived down the block on 6th Street—to dance for hours to Prince and Michael Jackson's "Off The Wall." Sliding across our make-believe dance floor in slippers, heads falling back in laughter as we adorned the room with rings of smoke, I forgot about the world.

It felt good to be bad—not caring about my grades, not caring about making the right choices all the time, not being told what to do. I was lonely, in a sense, and looking for love, but other parts of my life felt liberating. I didn't care about my academics but I went out of my way to read books by authors like James Baldwin, Toni Morrison, and Jean Toomer. I skipped enough school senior year for Friends to demand that I show up on senior cut day—an annual tradition—otherwise I'd risk the possibility of graduating. I attended feeling somewhat embarrassed but without much regret. Skipping school helped me escape the internal pressures I felt to be a good girl. It also helped me reach for the Black woman that I was seeking to become. There were parts of me that sometimes wanted to take even bigger risks, but I knew that I was ultimately the one who would have to pull myself out. So, I only flirted with danger.

However, in that stretch of time between day and night, when night seemed to last for hours in the haze of weed and alcohol, another part of me emerged. A howling, wild part. I heard myself. I laughed uncontrollably and my laugh was contagious. I unleashed parts of my imagination that even surprised me. I was uninhibited, unapologetic, fiery and "so fucking funny," my friends would always say. It probably did nothing to strengthen my immune system (unless you count the effects of bellyaching laughter), but I wouldn't take back those bad girl escapades for anything.

SMOKE AND MIRRORS

Is anybody there?
any?
Body?
Any recognizable shape?
Anyone to hold?
To hold me
Any familiar   someone?

Is it just smoke and mirrors?
Figments of my mind
Thick and opaque
Like time

Is anybody there?
Dance with me
I want you to dance with me
Dance with someBody
Let me pretend
That who I'm seeing
In the mirror is a friend
And not just thin air

Your Souls Music

VOICE LOG #72

You've been speaking this language since forever...
you just need a reminder.

FI NAN BOIS

"Moin ce fi nan bois
Moin ce fiq gain loa
Moin ce fiq qui vagnan.[23]"

—Frantz Casseus

I can still hear the melody and Creole lyrics to "Fi Nan Bois" in my head: "I am the girl of the woods, I have a good spirit, I am a girl who is strong." It's been decades since a friend and guitarist at Oberlin, David Hyman, asked me to sing this duet by the Haitian composer, Frantz Casseues Casseus, but that tune has stuck with me ever since. Looking back, I realize how this song has been like a metaphor for discovering my path in music. When I was in college, I often felt like a fish out of water. Oberlin was abundant with stimulating academics, but there were also myriad ways to get lost.

I could get lost in scholarly and theoretical African American studies courses, or I could absorb myself in pulsating dance electives. I could get lost and fall into the hollows of poetry in the creative writing group I was a part of, or the metaphysics of meditation in the group I started with a spiritual counselor. I could get lost in the genius, kindness and generosity of my advisor, professor and author Calvin Hernton, who—from our very first meeting—made me feel that I mattered

---

23   Casseus, Frantz. "Fi Nan Bois." *Haitiana*. Afro-Carib Records, 1971.

and belonged. But I felt most bewildered when I was amongst the page-turning, scarf-swishing, and rhythm-conducting music students of the conservatory.

So it came as quite a relief (tinged with notes of anxiety) when David asked if I would present two songs with him by Casseus: "Fi Nan Bois" and "Meci Bon Die[24]." I had performed maybe once within the confines of the conservatory at a mini- recital for beginning voice students. For singers with little to no western classical voice training, the only way to receive voice lessons was to first study with a voice major at the conservatory, and then gradually be promoted to working with a professor.

I began studying classical voice with a student named Derrick Gay—a tall Black countertenor who was as passionate about voice as traveling and studying foreign languages. He was part of a small group of Black voice students, many of whom became close friends of mine. Singers like Sibyl, a statuesque Black woman with a beautiful round voice, who would later sing with me as a backup singer on my first European tour and become a lifelong friend. These students—being opera singers—all had big voices, hearty laughs, and quick wits. Their brazen mouths and ability to stand in multiple realities and identities drew me near. Although I wasn't as passionate or trained in classical singing, the students could relate to my connections to jazz, R&B, funk, and soul, even if it wasn't being taught much at the conservatory.

Like pretty much all beginning voice students, at the time I had to study songs from *Twenty-Four Italian Songs and Arias*[25]—a collection of twenty-four songs that have become standard repertoire for early voice students. While I thought the songs were fun, I also felt *way* outside of my comfort zone. I had dipped my toes into perhaps one song or two when I was in voice class during high school, but the expectation then was merely to sing the song as best you could, with feeling, without

---

24   Casseus, Frantz. "Meci Bon Die." *Haitiana.* Afro-Carib Records, 1971.

25   *Twenty-Four Italian Songs and Arias.* (New York: G. Schirmer, 1948.)

running out of air, and to put some feeling in it. At the conservatory, the bar was significantly raised. Good breathing, articulation, accurate pronunciation, and feeling were required.

Most of the singers there had been studying classical music for years prior to arriving at college. I felt inadequate and far from my musical home—far from improvisation, edgy Soul and the scrappy kind of collaboration where the best possibilities for my voice and musical expression could reveal themself. With the music of Frantz Casseus, at least I could connect to more of my own interests in Black, folk artists. Casseus was not only a Black composer but being Haitian, he wove the traditional, folk music of Haiti into his writing. However, the songs were still classical in nature, so I needed help preparing them.

Fortunately, I had Derrick's help to coach me through the music while David worked steadily on learning his guitar parts. David was petite, with a timid nature, dark brown hair, and a beard, which he often stroked as he did his guitar when he was in thought. He wore glasses and spoke quietly, often smirking when his ideas escaped his mouth. He was a guitarist, jazz lover, and a student of ethnomusicology and music education. Even though David and I were quite different, it was clear to me that he too had a musical hunger for something broader and more encompassing than what the conservatory was presenting at that time.

Music classes at the conservatory were highly rigorous in theory, history, and performance, but there were almost no music classes offered in the subjects of songwriting or genres like free jazz, funk, gospel, R&B, or rock. There were also no jazz voice teachers, and NO jazz voice major! So, what was a girl like me to do?

I did what many do. I tried to find my way through the music that was available to me. Derrick, my student teacher, and I met regularly as he helped lead me through vocal exercises to stretch my range and improve my breath support so I could meet the highs, lows, and haunting intimacy of the music. He encouraged me like my later voice professor, Mr. Anderson, to produce that quintessential vibrato which classical singers are known for. Although I was faking it, it was preferred and celcorated by all the teachers and students alike (which seemed strange to me, and later became part of my impetus for studying vocal technique).

David and I rehearsed—searching to find our musical connection to one another and the material until it was time to perform. I performed for my second concert in the auditorium. Although my breath and tone still needed improvement, I had built a little more confidence and gained some new singing skills. As I sang those two compositions, I could feel my voice quake with nervousness, but also something new—a desire and devotion to do the songs justice.

But that was just the tip of the iceberg. Over the years, "Fi Nan Bois" was secretly working its magic on me. As my time at Oberlin progressed, I continued to wrestle with where I fit in amongst classical music majors and jazz instrumentalists. Afterall, there were only two other singers with interests in jazz like myself—Cathy Elliot, a composer and singer, and Rashida Philips, a vocalist with a deep, rich voice akin to a Sarah Vaughn. But without a voice mentor in jazz and Black American music, I was often left scrambling to create well- matched opportunities for myself. I zig zagged between dance and music, and dance and African American studies, until I decided that if I was going to stay at Oberlin, I needed to create my own major. One that allowed me to fully pursue my areas of interest.

I attempted to put this all into words in a proposal for a new major. Oberlin, being an open- minded institution, already had offered an option for students to write their own majors. I made it to round one of offering my proposal, and it was denied. The jury saw holes in my vision, which they asked me to revise. However, those holes only fed my self-doubts and my confidence to write my own independent major withered. Why was I spending so much time trying to justify a major that I would only be in for two years? I threw my hands up and opted for a more conventional major which already existed. I chose an emphasis in music through the college (instead of the conservatory), as this meant I would need fewer music credits to graduate and could still study other subjects through the college. My focus was in music theory and music history—(ironically, two areas I was the least interested in and felt the least confident). But given my level of experience in classical music, it was the most accessible to me.

The one thing which my chosen major lacked was the opportunity to actually sing—imagine that. So, I found opportunities to perform at coffeehouses, in student dance concerts, and here and there as a guest with the jazz big band if they performed a number that required a vocalist. I also danced with Dance Diaspora, the African dance company at Oberlin. But by far the most fulfilling moment in my performing life at Oberlin came when I decided to create my own concert with music and dance entitled, *Fi Nan Bois*.

Finally, the girl in the woods was finding a voice. I started sifting through recordings in the library to select the music I wanted to feature—songs that I often used to console myself and daydream to between blurry music assignments. I called on the memories of dances my mom and her friends choreographed downtown in community gardens—dance theater pieces I watched the Urban Bush Women develop. Bit by bit I assembled a collection of songs that had been most meaningful to me during my years of study. Then I wrote and gathered pieces of my own prose to link the music together. And finally, I found a like-minded cast of singers, musicians, and dancers to join me in this undertaking.

My main partner in crime was my dear friend and choreographer, Ana Maria Alvarez. She and I had the genius idea to perform a double bill for our senior concerts. The shows ran for several nights, alternating between her dance performance and my music-theater performance. Depending on whose night it was, there was always a section which featured guest dancing or singing in the other's performance.

In the pitch black of scene changes, our group of singers would emerge singing "Yes You[26]" by Bobby McFerrin. An ensemble of five voices would cut through the amaretto lights, and then suddenly, Ana

26   Bobby McFerrin. "Yes You." *Medicine Music*. 1990.

and her dancers would begin to captivate the audience with their swirling and bopping hips, arms, and legs. On other nights, my cast and I would joyously begin the same song as dancers would spill down the stairs, legs and arms wrapping over banisters, surprising the audience in celebration. It was at this time that I first chose to take on the Ornette Coleman composition, "What Reason," which my music brother and trumpeter, Kevin Louis, helped me to transcribe. We sat for hours in the living room at The African Heritage House pressing play and rewind, over and over, attempting to parcel out musical lines to give out to the cast.

I still have this performance saved on a VHS tape somewhere in my apartment. For years I kept the announcement flyer, too—a black and white photo of Ana and I dressed in retro 70s outfits. Bell bottoms, and shirts with oversized collars flopping, hats balanced boldly yet immaturely with unlit cigars in hand, posed to take on anyone who dared to challenge us. Everything had been executed using the full scope of our imaginations and resources. Of course, it was emulative at times, but we gave it our all and that enthusiasm and comradery was our strength.

Recently, my friend Sibyl, who sang in the show, was visiting with another Oberlin alum, Michael Preacely, now a doctor in vocal performance, choir leader, father, and husband. As they caught up on each other's lives, he told Sibyl how fun that show had been so many years ago. At the time, his would-be-wife had come to visit Oberlin and saw our presentation of *Fi Nan Bois*. She remarked how seeing all those creative Black students, singers, musicians, writers, and dancers, making art together had been a key factor in her decision to choose Oberlin for college. I never knew that my little play had made such a big impact. Even if my voice was nervously, yet joyfully, quaking at times, it seemed that my vision was stronger than any of my concerns.

MY OWN CLIMB

"But scientists decided long ago that plants were deaf and mute, locked in isolation without communication. The possibility of conversation was summarily dismissed. Science pretends to be purely rational, completely neutral, a system of knowledge-making in which the observation is independent of the observer... Tree conversations are still far above our heads.[27]"

—ROBIN WALL KIMMERER

When I was born, it felt as if all the trees in the forest were taller than me. Tall trees with broad limbs and long trunks and leaves that shimmered. They would dance and make music in the night until Grandmother Moon would appear, and even until Sun would come back from his long journey. Even though they were not great, great big trees, as big as Sycamore or wise Oak, they were still taller than I, and so I always had to look up to see them. It made me happy and proud to be with them, but a little scared and excited, too.

My friends and I were all bushes and saplings—or so we thought. We would giggle and laugh in the morning before our parents woke. We made up songs, pretending to be Sunderland, Pine, Pinchot. Making our voices imitate the different curves and slurs, funny jabs and inflections that their voices made when they sang. Even when we weren't trying to be tall trees, there was always someone to remind us that we had grown

27   Robin Wall Kimmerer, *Braiding Sweetgrass* (Minneapolis: Milkweed Editions, 2013.)

up in the same forest. Some Maple or Elm would reach its branch down to see us and say how similar our leaves were to our parents', how familiar the surface of our bark looked. So much so that they didn't even have to see us from the front, they could tell just by the way we bent and how our branches and leaves ascended similarly to our mothers and fathers.

Growing up, we all wanted to rise and shine. Like the day Spruce's branches began to widen like Eagle's. His leaves started to flap and flicker like the wings of many sparrows. In his first season of blooming as a tall tree, his bark showed new shades of brown, and with deeper crevices than before. His branches reached far beyond what our eyes could see. But not every tree is destined to be a tall one. Yet all of us saplings and bushes would wiggle with excitement in the hopes for our turn to grow like Spruce.

What we didn't know was that some of us were never going to be tall trees. Some of us would always stay low to the ground, low where Rabbit and Squirrel live. Low where Snake and Lizard crawl, where Rabbit and Squirrel hide their store of gifts and litters of children for winter. Where Fox stops to smell for their leftovers to see if they have forgotten anything, or anyone. Down low where Sparrow and her sisters hide inside and make us look like short women with singing bosoms. Some of us would always stay close to Creek and River, close enough to hear her water rippling down sister rocks. We were the ones who could hear the messages that Deer would leave for her other family members.

Pine, Maple, Sunderland—they got to hear the conversations of all the birds. Crow, and Robin, and Woodpecker tapping morse code on their sides. The taller trees—they would make their music from the things up high, from the shape of the clouds, the songs of the wind. And the only beings from the ground who they would listen to were those with the loudest and strongest voices, like Wolf. That is why we all thought we had to sound like Wolf just to be heard. To make our voices so strong that even Grandmother Moon would hear us. Little did we know that she always heard us.

But there was one place where all of us, trees and saplings, listened as much as we talked—in the Down Below. Down Below was where all saplings, tall trees, and wise trees would commune. There, everyone's voice had strength, regardless of their height or the rings of their trunk. In the Down Below, no tree was more important than another. We all needed each other equally. Each tree had to lend its roots for support so that we might all survive. From Down Below, we spread messages, warnings of disease, winter and frost, and sweets for filling our stems and making our flowers bloom. From Sycamore, I learned not to eat too quickly, to save what he had given so that when winter came, I would have strength during the cold months. From Pine I learned to share with other trees and bushes so we could all be fed. And I learned that I could teach others to listen to one another, because even as a small tree, there are certain things that tall trees cannot understand. Down Below we held hands, nourished the weak, fended off ailments, and always sought new ideas for how to grow closer to the sun.

Every fourth ceremony, Grandmother Moon would appear to tell a story to all the forest. It was at this time that Fox would not torment Rabbit, that Squirrel and Chipmunk stopped fighting, and Snake would sit and listen without commenting. It was then that the tall trees, and those of us closer to the ground, would all listen to hear what wisdom Grandmother had to share.

I remember the day Grandmother told us the story of River and Ocean. River had always loved to dance through the forest. Her love of travel and curiosity made her a good runner and easy to talk to since she was accustomed to meeting so many new plants and animals on her journeys. However, the first time she saw Ocean, she realized that she had set her sights too small. Ocean was immense, as large as the sky—so big and powerful to River that she seemed infinite. She impressed River with her beautiful, large waves that curved upwards, and her ability to change rock's minds and move entire schools of fish, or even someone even as big as Whale. Suddenly, River felt small and embarrassed that her adventures seemed childlike compared to Ocean's sophistication.

River wanted to be powerful, too. But how could she be? River was long and wide at times, but small compared to Ocean. River didn't make large impressions the way Ocean did, or so she thought. What River failed to realize was that while she was off dancing and gallivanting through the forest, plants and animals were singing her praises too. They were celebrating her sweet taste—the freshness that she brought, the arrival of renewed soil, and new plants. The nourishment for baby fawns and frogs alike to grow. River didn't know that she was a weaver, a great connector, something that even Ocean depended upon. River could bring news from mountain tops all the way to Ocean and the Down Below. She had forgotten to see her own power. When Grandmother Moon said this, everyone stopped what they were doing, because as usual everyone had stopped fully listening (which is why Grandmother talks so slow and often repeats herself), but when Grandmother Moon said this we all listened because we remembered how special River was to all of us.

Although I had not finished growing, I then wondered if maybe my height might not be the best of me. I looked around the forest at all the bushes and saplings, the tall trees and wise trees, at all the animals and how different we were, yet how well we fit together. Deer needed Acorn just as much as Acorn needed Deer; and Rabbit needed Clover in the same way that we needed Rabbit to nourish the Down Below. And then I realized that maybe my voice didn't need to be as loud as Wolf's in order to be heard. That maybe the rings around my trunk might not need to be so numbered in order for me to be remembered and loved. And that is when I stopped trying to grow like Spruce, and instead started my own climb.

BELOW THE SURFACE

When I breathe low   and I remember
The way I was   before
The form   and formless
The way I was   and who I am
under the sun

Memory and muscle   as one
Breathing below   the surface
Memory and muscle   as one
Breathing below   the surface

THE SIDELINES

People are going to sit on the sidelines
Noticing that you forgot to add a comma
That your voice cracked
That the lyric was cliche
or didn't rhyme

But, it's much easier to sit on the sidelines

SACRED MUSIC, BEYOND THE NOTES

Whether on a subway platform or in a concert hall, music gets up close and personal, and there, everything becomes sacred. When I was in high school, I fell in love with the sound of the electric guitar, and a particular man who played one. When he played, I could hear all the stories of his life. I could hear his loneliness, his strength, his wit, his awkwardness, his sadness, his darkness, and his desire to break free. To break free from the confines of race, gender, and class. I could hear all the desires he had, and which most everyone had at some point, including me, a young Black girl from NYC, jumping to and fro in search of her own reflection. Hopping from funk to ska to hip-hop and alternative shows in the 90s, I was looking for love, but I was also looking to find myself, my own beauty, and strength. Little did I know then that power can be found in the smallest and even most obscure places.

I grew up listening to the long tones and solos of my dad practicing flute and alto saxophone. His practice became (and still is like) the equivalent to the sounds of birds, trees rustling, a refrigerator's hum—the music of living. I regularly heard people rave and swoon over his music and or "genius." To me, my father's playing always sounded like words, like his speech. His voice and his playing became interchangeable with his loud laugh and idiosyncratic, and strong opinions. From a young age, I was absorbing sound beyond the notes.

No one explained to me when I was young what was going on musically, or why everyone was pursuing these creative ideas with such fervor. But I didn't need them to because the gatherings, rehearsals, and concerts spoke for themselves. Those rituals brought together different kinds of people—of different races, different styles, different sexes, languages, sexualities, and ages. They brought joy. They brought curiosity and conversation. They caused people to dance and let their bodies do the talking. They brought people to shout and nod in reflection and affirmation. They got people painting and writing poetry on the spot. They made people laugh. They made people cry. What else did I need to know? Clearly this was a good place, an important place. And that place was music itself.

Even though my parents didn't raise me in any organized religion, every artistic space I was in seemed to hold a reverence for art—whether it was music, dance, theater, visual art, or literature. They held particular esteem for taking things to the edge and stretching beyond the spoon-fed depictions of life and art. Even at my school there were teachers and mentors who encouraged me to find my voice and let it ring.

Linda Monseen, my voice and music teacher, made me feel my voice was special and worth developing. She taught me music and coached me, from kindergarten to through elementary school, high school, and after college. She introduced me to the music and extended vocal techniques of Meredith Monk. Bob Rosen, my jazz teacher, taught me the importance of swing, putting my spin on things, and keeping life and music fun. Daphne Taylor, my arts teacher, taught me to sew, draw, to study things around me, and trust my perspective, and appreciate my own interpretation. They, like all good teachers, were guiding me to develop consistency and also take risks. They demonstrated—both through their own creative pursuits and their teaching—the joy in life-long learning.

By the time I graduated from Oberlin, I had improved my skills in reading music and playing *some* notes on the piano. To get through many frustrating homework assignments, I had listened to jazz and classical recordings that broadened my music library, such as Charles Mingus' "Fables of Faubus.[28]" I had performed the music of Duke Ellington with the big band. I'd practiced in a jazz combo class with the

---

28   Charles Mingus. "Fables of Faubus." *Minus Ah Um. 1959.*

terror of saxophonist Donald Walden barking over at me. I had also studied African American poets with mentor-authors, Calvin Hernton and hattie gossett and I had taken African American studies courses with professors and personal bedrocks like visual artist Johnny Coleman and director, Caroline Jackson-Smith.

By the time I left Oberlin, I was hungry to bring my artistic voice forward without the prerequisites of any class or professor. I wanted to explore what I knew to be true—that thing I had been searching for in high school while gallivanting from the Knitting Factory to CBGB's to the Cutting Room. I wanted to sing music irrespective of what genre it fit into.

After a few years of getting my bearings in New York City, things started feeling like they were coming together. I started my time living with my dad and stepmom after college, and slept in a bed with my little sister, before moving to a fifth-floor walkup on Second Avenue just a few blocks away. My fairy godmother, Laurie Carlos, had swooped in to save me again, helping me find an apartment just in the nick of time.

I had gone from commuting two hours each way working for a textbook publishing company in Westchester, (where my close friend's mom, Barbara, worked) to then working for a high-end jewelry company. I began my employment in public relations at Me & Ro, where I loaned out lavish jewelry to magazines and celebrities, like Mary J Blige, for photoshoots. I later moved to working in retail at their first brick and mortar location while attending the Institute for Audio Research.

I was unwinding and at the same time rooting myself deeper in my interests. Unlike many of my classmates, I had graduated from Oberlin without a plan. (I had similarly entered Oberlin without *confirming* that my intended plan was even possible.). I felt a bit like I was playing catch-up. It wasn't until things in my personal and financial life started taking a toll on me that I decided to look for a more drastic pivot. That's when I landed a job working for Peace Bisquit, a boutique music management company run by manager, DJ, and producer, Bill Coleman.

Bill knew a close family friend and music producer named Brian

Bacchus. I interviewed with Bill at his apartment in Clinton Hill, Brooklyn, and got the job. For the next three years of my life, things changed for the better. It was only a few weeks after starting my job as a personal assistant that I met an unassuming, handsome guy who would become my future husband.

I landed my first long term music residency shortly after I started working for Bill. This became the music opportunity I had been craving. It gave me the space to try out new ideas and transform them into something holy. Every other Sunday, at a small hole-in-the-wall cafe around the corner from my apartment on Second Avenue, I would sing for three hours a night. The place was called the Anyway Cafe. It kind of felt like that, too. You could have been anywhere in the world really— such a small, unassuming spot with live music every night of the week.

There I would play there with my accompanist at the time, a cellist named Dana Leong. Listening to my roommate, Grisha—a dancer; choreographer; and art maker—using bits of cello in her vocal theater group (Hot Mouth, co-founded with former Urban Bush Woman, Viola Sheeley), had inspired me to explore the pairing of voice and cello. My first collaborator, Shiao-shu, had been the younger sister of my childhood friend Ha-chi. We didn't get to play many gigs together, but we did lay some groundwork for how to play together. My second cellist broke his collarbone playing football, and that's when I sought out a recommendation from my dad and wound up working with Dana. I had mostly been exploring covers. The music we played was basically like performing a Pyeng mixtape. The requirements went something like this: "Do I love this song? Do I like this song?... Then we should do it!"

There in that tiny underground restaurant, we covered songs by, or made famous by, artists like Björk, Bill Withers, Nat King Cole, Chaka Khan, Ella Fitzgerald, and others. I felt encouraged by singers like Nina Simone and later, Cassandra Wilson, who broke down the rules about what a jazz singer was "supposed" to do. I was trying to define myself as an artist.

After cello, I later moved to more traditional accompaniment, working with a guitarist named Ryan Scott, who Dana introduced me to. Ryan and Dana became staple players in my first band. Ryan had an immediately tangible soulfulness to his playing and he could sing. He'd moved to New York City from Carmel, California as a young singer-songwriter, straight out of high school, seeking to pursue his craft. I performed at the Anyway Cafe every other weekend and it became a primary ingredient, not only for me, but also for my small congregation of friends and family.

Similar to my evening sets, the menu at the Anyway Cafe was small, but intentional. It wasn't a fancy place, but they put effort into what they had. The drinks at the cafe were centered around a variety of vodkas infused with lychee or raspberry, while the menu played off their French-Russian theme—sweet and savory crepe dishes, stewed beef or chicken stroganoff, or their famous beet salad with goat cheese.

Some evenings there would be only one person who would come to sit and listen to the music. (On many Sundays, that one person was my boyfriend.) Other nights there might be a surprisingly rowdy table in the corner, or a group of my friends who would stop by to lush it up, clap, and sing along with the songs that had become our "hits." We would step outside together for cigarette breaks and bond with the various bartenders. Some evenings, a friend would bring a new companion, partner, or family member, or someone visiting from out of town, and then later share how my gig had been one of the highlights of their trip.

The place being so small it somehow helped to bottle the magic of that time. The magic of being in our early twenties, without the responsibilities of children and spouses, and without the greater responsibilities of making money.

It sounds a bit simple and unglamorous—performing for a room of mostly empty tables in a not-so-well- lit restaurant, on a dirty side street below street level—but Anyway had a charm. It became a hallowed place because of its inhabitants and the music we brought with us. Our sacred relics were a cello, markings on staff paper, a microphone, amplifier, a voice, and the sounds of laughter and glasses clinking. The charm came from all of us, musicians and audience, sitting side by side. Some nights the cafe was completely full, and we could have stayed there way past closing; and other nights were blistering cold outside, with no one but my boyfriend sitting in the corner.

Even on those nights where there were only a couple tables of diners, something magical would happen with just one song, an ending, or a solo that Dana or I would take. He would sometimes find a groove with his loop pedal (something new for the times), or create a musical atmosphere where we would just linger. It taught us how to drop into the music no matter the circumstances, no matter the stakes. How to suss out the energy of the crowd, how to draw from our own energy, no matter what we were feeling. That's when we would discover the little things—a vocal tone, a vamp, where to leave silence.

To this day, people tell me how much those memories of us playing at Anyway meant to them. I'm sure our age and energy multiplied the effect. Something in that room helped me connect to the sacred in the sublime. In later years, I would go on to perform for hundreds of people on the coast of San Sebastian, Spain, in Cognac, France, Sardinia, Italy and for thousands in Montreal where there were so many people I could hardly focus any one person's face. It was electric and truly transcendental. But there's also a trembling vulnerability and intimacy when performing in front of just ten people. In the casual light of someone's living room, or beside a beaten-up bar at a café—there I could display the stories of my life. I could present my yearning, my loneliness, my strength, wit, awkwardness, sadness, darkness, and my desire to break through and free myself from any and everything trying to disrupt me.

DEAD LEAVES

Dead leaves
These are dead leaves
Old things
That crackle and crunch
Things that bunch up and curl at the edges
They used to give to me

Dead leaves
These things have no blood left
No color
They don't hold water
They no longer have the strength to stand
Always with their heads hanging limp

These are old things
Things that don't bloom or blossom
Like vampires and nightmares they lose their might in the sun
Withering, melting
No way to feed them now
No purpose mourning them

Dead leaves
These things are breaking under my feet
Crunching like snow and firecrackers
Celebratory steps reminding me
They are losing their strength

Finally all these leaves
Are breaking down
Turning into microscopic versions of themselves
Puzzle pieces with nowhere to go
And staring at fertility now I've forgotten what ever used to be

LEARNING HOW TO LISTEN

Recently my family and I rented a cottage upstate in Marlboro, NY. The place had a more 1980s "ugly sweater" vibe and damp carpets than we had thought from the Airbnb pictures, but the listing price was nearly half of anything else we found online in the heat of July. Plus, the notion of having a country house for an entire month was a luxury beyond anything we could afford in the past. We arrived in Marlboro in our Tiguan, loaded with instruments, a few of my husband's wood sculptures, computers, backpacks, and a puppy recovering from knee surgery.

I was still thrilled to be there. We met the owner of the Airbnb while she was cutting grass on a *Duke's of Hazard*-style lawn mower. She didn't notice us approaching at first, as she listened to the music inside her giant headphones. A shorter, solid- looking woman of French-Canadian descent with blonde hair, she and her husband had recently bought their home, the large house on the property, along with the smaller cottage. They were still settling into the main house. With lumber and furniture supplies being severely backed up due to the pandemic, they were living without a couch and several other basic items. It was funny to imagine this young couple in their expansive home with only a few pieces of furniture and their tiny, white yipping dog.

The backorder on furniture helped explain the oversized, slightly sunken L-shaped couch installed on the second floor loft of our cottage. With dark, swirling colors and chenille throw pillows that didn't match, it felt like this couple hadn't done much to upgrade the space from the previous owners. There was a large tv, and a heavy, round wooden coffee table, with a bed situated across from it, and draping curtains to create privacy. In a corner near some of the windows, there were two chairs and a barrel with a wooden top to dine at. There was a nice nook beside the couch with a desk and shelves. Some nostalgic vintage video games had also been added to entertain guests.

I looked at everything and thought that there needed to be some changes, but I could work with it. On the side of the house, there was an official bedroom with a full, metal-framed bed and cutesy wallpaper. Looking at it, the bedroom felt inviting, as if the wife had put extra effort into decorating. However, once lying down, the faults quickly revealed themselves—when my head and upper body slid backwards between the bars of the headboard. The room was bright and there was a lot of natural light. There was an unused garage, which the wife had turned into her furniture upcycling studio, and generously offered to my husband to work on his sculptures. Overall the house had a workable, albeit clammy, kind of charm. (My teenage daughter, on the other hand, felt strongly otherwise!).

Living in a rather flimsy cottage for nearly an entire month, we began feeling the effects of the outside world steadily seep into our interior world. Even if we didn't spend loads of time outside (for reasons I will explain), I still noticed how the smell of dew in the morning seemed to settle my mind. The rushing creek and tussling hedgehogs became my new entertainment, and the sunshine, rain, and of course, insects were our new obsession.

We were quite wary of the insects, specifically the ticks, as our neighbor in Brooklyn had recently contracted Lyme disease and his speech and movements had dramatically slowed down, like someone twice his age. The shock of seeing his rapid transformation had terrified both my husband and me, so we developed a daily ritual for each and every time we walked our dog: put on your socks, pull them up, Pippy Longstocking-style, to the knees; spray your legs and feet with tick spray; then spray the dog (who would fearfully resist the unknown spritzing creature); slip on our shoes and venture on as brief a walk as possible. The irony wasn't lost on us—we had rented a house in the country and were scared to fully dip our toes in the grass. But our fears and limited walks couldn't keep us from being touched by the natural world. There was a palpable difference between being outnumbered by trees versus brick buildings, between hearing the wind and rain versus hearing car horns and blaring music.

My husband helped me to relocate my desk, keyboard and laptop to a seat near the window so that I could stare at the massive rolling lawn while writing and teaching. Despite the dimly lit kitchen with its mysterious smells, lopsided oven, and dank carpet, from there in that upstairs corner I found a little slice of heaven. Moments of stillness in which I could absorb the peace that summer greenery imparts.

It reminded me of a book I started reading excerpts from about twelve years ago called *The Listening Book*, by W.A. Mathieu. The Listening Book is a collection of invitations and instructions for hearing oneself and the world around you. I learned about it from an old Oberlin classmate and drummer in my California band, Micha Patri. I think it wasn't until returning to New York, several years later, when I actually started reading passages and considering the practices like this one:.

"Rain.
River; waterfall.
Crickets; FROGS.
Wind around corners.
Your own breathing.
People hammering at a construction site: the cross rhythms.[29]"

To some this may seem a bit trivial, to be an actual listening lesson but for many of us, especially musicians, know that our ears are one of our greatest assets. Training your ears to listen is not just about deciphering bass lines, trumpet solos, lyrics, or intervals; it's also about learning how to expand your depth of hearing to take in sounds near and far, loud and soft, left and right, musical, industrial, ambient, and even physical.

---

29   W.A. Mathieu, *The Listening Book: Discovering Your Own Music* (Boulder: Shambala Publications, 1991.)

In some ways, it is arguably a different state of being.

In the Alexander Technique, we also learn new ways of being. We focus on re-educating our minds and bodies in order to shift habitual physical and mental patterns that often create tension—such as a stiff neck, tendonitis, lower back pain, TMJ, and anxiety—to create greater ease in the body and mind. To do this, there is a great emphasis on self-observation. It's like waking meditation, or what is referred to as mindfulness, but with the added awareness of one's physical alignment. Self-observation can go something like this: as you tune in to your breath, your mind and body become less rushed. You notice the possibility for ease along the length of your neck and spine, and perhaps your vision expands, and the tension around your eyes softens. You take a new inhale and feel your arms resting at your sides. Instead of gripping your hands and feet, you start to relax and open, letting your weight ripple down through to the earth. The tricky part is to continue the practice without expecting a set result. Repeating this level of self-observation on a daily basis begins to ingrain awareness as its own ritual which, for many, creates a kind of self-expansion and relief from physical tension and mental stress. In much the same way that I practice listening to my body, I learned to listen more closely to sounds of all kinds—waterfalls, crickets and frogs.

In diving into a deeper kind of listening, the kind that sound therapists, as well as healers, and creative music makers have centered on, you can access another way to hear the emotion, or heart, of music. The intention and desired connection musicians are making with the audience and the energy of the room. With expansive listening you start to listen to the way that players listen to one another too. There's a living conversation, or ecosystem, within a band. A drummer's brushes grace their cymbals in response to a bass fill in response to a vocalist's quick rhythmic flutter. Similarly, there's a whole conversation happening in the world—and not just the natural world, but the industrial, slogging, banging, screeching world, as well.

Living in a city like New York, it's not often that you encounter frogs or waterfalls (depending on your location) but there is a tremendous amount of construction, planes, and rumbling subways. These sounds create their own "symphony," according to Mathieu. Although it can become grating at times, inspiring someone like myself to need a weekend getaway, there are other days when I hear the music in it. If I allow myself to settle in, I can use the sounds of the city to tune back into myself and vice versa.

It's somewhat of a double- consciousness that you have to build being a musician and a New Yorker, to hear the music and quiet the negative at the same time. But reading W.A. Mathieu's book and studying the Alexander Technique made me want to open my relationship to what was around me whether surrounded by rolling hills or skyscrapers. What if there was something to embrace in the industrial organs of Brooklyn, Manhattan, Queens, and the Bronx? If I really sat quietly I could hear the songs of plants just as well as the songs of people.

Abbey Lincoln has a song entitled "Learning How To Listen." In the chorus she states:

"I'm learning how to listen
How to hear a melody
How to hear the song I'm singing
How to feel and let it be
Listen for the song
Knowing how it goes
And listen to the melody that flows[30]"

Even from that funny little cottage on a sloping hill, perched on my chair, staring out the window—I too was learning how to listen.

---

30   Lincoln, Abbey. "Learning How to Listen." *Wholly Earth.* Verve Records, Gitanes Jazz Productions, 1998.

LOOSENING MY TONGUE

It was decided before I was brought to my mother
(The one who danced)
Before I was brought to this plane
Where all the plants, animals and insects were divided into strange
groupings,
Where they each spoke in a different tongue,
(And humans pretend to conduct nature like an orchestra)
Though it already plays effortlessly.
It was decided amongst the older women,
The Great Great Conjurers
They whispered with their backs to her,
(To me as well)
Old songs and text,
Hymns flapping between them.
Tired and proud mothers,
Loving and resentful wives
They decided I would be their voice
And without asking,
Without me knowing
A woman with heavy breasts slipped something into my mouth.
I was too young to understand the taste of cold and the burn of spice
The peculiar feeling that it left in my mouth
And the fire that it put in my belly
Something between sweet peaches and hot peppers,
Yet unsettling like bitter herbs.

It stayed with me all the while traveling to my mother.
As I swam through dark canals with strange sounds,
I heard her voice reverberating through the waterways
Sounding angrier and more scared than I had ever known her to be.
During that time my mother was the most foreign to me.
I feared the Great Great Conjurers had taken her away,
Swapping me with another child who would rest in the comfort of my
old home
As I was fed to a new woman posing as my mother.
(A mean and hardened woman)
Leaving me to starve.

I felt my mother's insides tired from moving me.
I had grown so happy in my home,
The nest the Great Great Conjurers had sent me to
Where life had been safe and simple.
Day and night were always one
And all nourishment came to me without asking.
If ever my mother became forgetful all I had to do was
(Kick, kick, kick),
And then she would quite swiftly meet my request
Lulling me back to my dreamy slumber.

My life before was like a hammock,
Rhythmic and easy.
The only thing missing was a view but since I had not known sight, I
could not miss it.
I had everything one could ask for.
It was only in arriving on this plane that I had to learn so many new
ways.

It began as a moan
One long moan after another
Deep and resounding
Trailing over mountains and hills
Men came out of their houses,
People stopped working,
Cooking,
Building,
To see what unfamiliar noise
That was.
And from moans it became a growl
That's when I knew this was what The Great Great Conjurers had given
me
Their grievances started to pour out of me like vomit,
Like an uncontrollable sickness.
It was as if the taste which they had planted in my mouth
So many dimensions ago had finally soured then burst
And brought with it the years and eras of their abused lives, solitude,
loneliness and triumph.

They had given it to me with no instructions
For there were no instructions for what they had witnessed
Nor what they had dreamed.
Their voices went through me like flames
Burning vegetation,
Scattering small animals,
Moving large rocks.
Canyons split wider
Water dove deeper
The people held each other in fear
My body trembling and sweating
Yet then it exploded like a fresh reservoir bubbling from a dark place
Watering the scorched patches of earth around me

My stomach still heaving
Ululations spread from my mouth
Waking all night creatures
All timekeepers stopped
Everyone waited quieting their breath
So as not to disrupt mine any further.

Days and nights passed.
Night and day,
From sunrise to sunset
The people tried helplessly to sleep
But their bodies could not avoid
The sound of my voice ringing in their ears
I too barely slept.
And then an unfamiliar feeling moved inside me
The pit which had always been there became smaller
And then smaller
And with its shrinking so too did my voice simmer
Gradually changing into a sweetened call.
Suddenly it's jagged knife of flames
Began melting the hearts of all those around.
Men began to weep
Women danced.
Low and softened
My voice escaped
Sweeping through homes
High and soaring
It covered rooftops.
The infirm began to walk,
Friends and foes embraced,
Children squealed with delight, playing once more.
Finally everyone sighed
Just as each of my limbs sighed

For the first time I took a breath and moved from where I sat
For what I thought had been months.
Yet when I looked in the mirror
I saw that I had aged decades.
But I no longer cared
My stomach no longer ached
And my voice,
My voice became a song of consolation
A song of redemption
A place of rest
A jubilant call
To rouse all wildlife and the people.
The Great Great Conjurers remind me
It's been completed,
That which they charged me with,
Has all spilled and dried over
And I am left with an exquisite taste
One that is saturated in honey and roses
Plum and wine.
Now I flap my tongue with a bright, boldness.
Savoring the tastes of time.

Staying Open & Open Again

VOICE LOG # 101

Sometimes I feel it, that all I have to do is just stay open and everything will be taken care of.

A POWERFUL VOICE: THE GOSPEL OF BLACK WOMEN

"Built on the power of our voices...
This music...
Built on the sound of Black women's voices.[31]"

—FAY VICTOR

If you're a Black singer who didn't grow up singing in the church, sometimes it can feel as if you're a bit of a unicorn. I can think of a number of Black performers from Whitney Houston to Mavis Staples to Aretha Franklin and more whose musical upbringing began in church. Black folks musical influence has been and continues to be one of our most profound contributions. As Black Americans, our music has impacted the entire planet, and gospel music in particular has been a musical rite of passage for many well well-known and successful artists.

Yet not every artist was raised within the church. I was talking to another student today, a Black woman performer, who brought up how out of place it can feel to be a Black singer who doesn't have the often expected gospel roots. Although it isn't the first time I've heard another singer say it, it's comforting, nonetheless, when I listen to other vocalists who have had a similar experience to mine. Church, especially church for Black folks, brings with it so many references to our culture, our

---

31   Victor, Fay. "Black Women's Music." Victor, 2021. Accesed May 24, 2023. https://www.fayvictor.com/compositions/black-womens-music-2020/

strength and life struggle in America.

The first time I heard "His Eye Is on the Sparrow," I was in college, and I quickly discovered the song's importance for the Black christian students on campus. Every time a student would sing it, they would transform, pouring their heart out, as their voices built into a crescendo, soaring higher and higher towards the sky. It was captivating and yet, I felt like I was missing an essential music element that others had. My version of "His Eye Is on the Sparrow" was Sarah Vaughn singing "Lullaby of Birdland," Laurie Carlos freely reciting poetry, and Sam Cooke wailing, "Darling you send me."

My parents grew up attending church. Their mothers and grandmothers brought them—squirming, giggling, pouting, singing—to honor the Lord every Sunday. Suits and dresses pressed, hair did. If I were to ask, they would likely know famed scriptures and hymns, which I do not know. They're accustomed to the rhythm of a sermon and the responsive choreography of a congregation. Fans fluttering, voices humming, bodies swaying. However, at this point, much of America is familiar with these signals. They exist as codes—which I absorbed in snippets from watching rehearsals with the Urban Bush Women, and which mainstream music, movies, and television have delivered to us because of their intrinsic nature to much of Black American life. I got church through African American dance and theater, and others received dance and theater through church.

The sermons I knew were the fiery scatting of Betty Carter and the sublime smokiness of Jeanne Lee's voice coasting through the air. I knew long-winded and persistent drum solos, blazing trumpets and raging saxophones. I knew Craig Harris' howling into his didgeridoo. I knew musicians dancing and dancers singing. I knew spoken poetry and sung stories. But my experience of church was a seasonal activity. Like catching fireflies or eating ice cream, my visits to church happened when the days were long and muggy.

Half my Sundays in July were spent at church with my paternal grandmother, Grandma Lillian. However, my biggest memory of going to church wasn't the ritual of turning pages or singing songs, but the ritual of getting dressed. Getting my hair pressed and curled, putting on stockings, slips and hot skirts with matching jackets, or blouses and tight patten leather shoes—hoping I wouldn't sweat my hair out too soon. I still have no idea what denomination Grandma Lillian was. Methodist? Baptist? Lutheran? I honestly couldn't even tell you the difference between the three. The same is true for my great- grandmother, Grandma Pierce. All I know is that her church was famed for its long- standing tradition of supporting famous reverends, singers, and politicians.

The other half of my July Sundays were spent at the Kingdom Hall. Most of my mother's siblings and their children were (and still are) Jehovah's Witnesses, except for my grandmother, Grandma Pearlie. Grandma Pearlie would often slide back and forth between her church and the Kingdom Hall (also between this world and others). Grandma was always going to do what she wanted to, and rarely wasted her breath explaining it to you. I saw what I thought were Grandma Pearlie's contacts with the spirit world in the silent episodes of her hands gesturing in the air. Like Thelonius Monk's onstage dances, she, too, was a whirling dervish. But no one mentioned those moments in relation to Jehovah.

Going to the Kingdom Hall was a ritual of great importance for my family, as suits, skirts, and hair were meticulously ironed for our arrival but, once gathered, it was a more solemn place. It was unique in that I would see people of different ethnic backgrounds: Black, White, Latino, Asian. That felt more akin to being home in New York. The enormity of the halls were sometimes so big it seemed like a basketball game or the next touring pop concert was about to start, but the service never built to that type of high. It was quite the opposite, as hundreds and hundreds of people sat in rows quietly flipping through the tissue paper Bibles and songbooks, holding their prayers. Being a Jehovah's Witness never caught my interest—even if Uncle Wayne, my Aunt Sheila's first husband, thought otherwise. He would talk and talk with such passion and fervor about Jehovah, sweating in the Georgian heat, repeatedly wiping his brow, I was compelled to listen. My Uncle Wayne liked to think that maybe my listening was a sign that I wanted to become a Witness, but I was more intrigued and, if anything, curious as to what could move him so.

I didn't know it then, but I would have jumped for gospel music had I been more exposed to it. The dramatic and full bodied expression of praise was everything my younger self already gravitated toward. I can just imagine how my eight-year-old self would have shimmied and shouted with the Spirit. Leaning into that deep howl and growl, yearning for that belting sound to blow through me—like the Blues, rock-n-roll and free jazz all rolled up into one. I can see my younger self feeling at home in the conviction and abandon of gospel music. The closest I got to that type of freedom was singing along to Chaka Khan belting "Through the Fire," or Tisha Campbell performing in Spike Lee's *"School Daze."* Later in life when I heard Aretha Franklin's recording of "Amazing Grace," and Amina Claudine Myers' "Have Mercy Upon Us," I knew what they were singing was real.

I think that's why my parents never wasted their breath telling me not to go to church. I was always going to receive a lesson whether I sat in a church or temple or listened to a trumpet solo. All while I was growing up, everyone felt adamant that *their* creation story and religious text was the *true* story of God, but they all sounded similar to me. I didn't see the need for arguing one over the other. All the principles to live by seemed mostly the same, with the united goal of finding a way to make it through the beauty and challenges of life gracefully.

I didn't grow up in church as most people know it but music and art were (and still are) my place of worship. As for the particulars of the ceremony, I could feel the Spirit all the time. I could feel it when my mother was dancing in a dusty dance studio; I could feel it when I was falling asleep on her lap at Sweet Basil's or The Village Vanguard; I could feel it in the passion of Aunt Laurie and Thought Music speaking poetry, eyes looking every way, I could feel it in my dad's sound on the saxophone; just as I can hear it echoing in the power of singers like The Clark Sisters, Patti LaBelle, and Jennifer Hudson.

A long time ago an ordinary man with an extraordinary sound came along and redefined the sound of the trumpet as we know it. His name was Louis Armstrong. Armstrong and many other musicians in jazz were said to have been emulating the sound of the human voice when they played through their instruments. From jazz to Blues to gospel those voices were and are the voices of Black women. The power in our voices has rippled over the planet and throughout music for decades. Irrespective of secular or sacred music Black women's voices are the roots and branches of so much music we listen to. They have influenced the masses and will likely continue to enrapture us for decades, if not, centuries to come.

HIDE AND SEEK

Are you really trying to *find* your voice? Can it really be found? How badly do you want it? And what would you be willing to release, or even shatter, in order to allow your little light to shine and become a big light? Who is hiding and who is playing seek?

At some point you made the choice to take music out on a date, show off your good side, take them to your favorite restaurant. Now it's been 6 six months and you're considering moving in, but you're not certain if this is what you really want. At every other turn, the directions are ambiguous, messages mixed, and the results mediocre. You're constantly being asked to bare blemishes and reveal old scars.

There's no exact timeline, no definitive answers. It may take a month, or a year, until you really feel like yourself. Practice regularly, yet don't over do it. Listen to other singers, but don't try to mimic their sound. Trust yourself, but make sure to ask for help.

Is all of this really necessary for finding your voice? A part of you that has *always* been a part of you, since birth (maybe even prior). So, perhaps it's not so much a finding as a clearing—a reconnecting, unwinding, and returning.

But there have still been those times when you weren't as confident, when you didn't raise your voice, speak your mind. When you muffled your requests, and hid your disappointment and desires.

It's *your* voice, but have you always been in control? Whether it was outside expectations, or those which you forced upon yourself. Your voice holds those impressions as well. And now, as you try to claim it, it seems that your voice insists you relinquish even more control!

Perhaps your voice has a will of its own, its own voice. What if your longing is merely a reflection of your deeper self wanting to be heard instead of ordered around? Wanting to be seen, not watched. What if it isn't you who's been doing the seeking, but actually your voice? What if it's some other part of you who's been hiding? Not that your hiding was without good reason. It took a great deal of skill. But let's imagine something new—let's imagine that now it's finally safe for you to be heard.

FIELDS OF IDEAS

Queens, NY, 11 AM

Saturday morning. An 8-year-old girl sits in her backyard wearing checker shorts, pink puffy socks, and a pink t-shirt. Her hair is in two afro puffs. She happily licks a cherry red lollipop in between talking and drawing chalk faces on the ground.

VIOLA

Pah! Grown-ups! How totally, completely, ridiculous are they? ...Pah! Abbbbsurd! I don't need anyone to tell me what to do. The only people who should be telling people what to do are the people without ideas—and I have LOTS of ideas! So, I don't need anyone telling me what to do. I have fields and fields of ideas. Freshly grown, whirling, curling, tons of ideas! Tons of ideas! Flowers of ideas. I don't need anyone to tell me what to do!

There isn't enough time to even play with them all. The ideas. Everyone is always interrupting me, trying to tell me something they want me to do, but I don't need to be interrupted with their "wah wah wah" boring ideas. All I need is time to play. Just give me time to play! And I will cook you up a grilled un-cheese with nutella and passion fruit pie.

VIOLA snaps her fingers.

It's always in season here. Everything is always in season.

Pick a season! Lots of roads to take. Lots of things to look at. Lots of vines to pull and shake.

> *VIOLA stands up gracefully gesturing to the garden like an airplane attendant.*

The vines are all over the place, but if you pick them up, one at a time, you can go anywhere you like. You can go dancing, trick or treating, you can write songs, or bake a cake, or sit on a tree top, or lie in the grass or in a boat and stare at the sky for as long as you like. As long as you like! And there are no grown-ups!

No grown ups.

There is tea and biscuits and there is always an endless supply of butter, and your choice of honey or fresh jam or even maple syrup. There are long train rides or boat rides. Basically, lots of time to look out the window—whichever kind of window you want—and daydream. You can choose your headphones or your favorite kind of silence. Quiet silence, or quiet quiet silence or sitting next to your best friend and drawing silence. You choose! And then we can go to London, or India, Bali, Mexico, or Africa, the south of France—but no matter where we are, you will always be warm. The sun will always be out and you can still have soft, fluffy sweaters to wear. Ahhhh! This place is perfect.

So many ideas to look at—phew!

> *VIOLA wipes her brow dramatically and sits back down.*

So many ideas to wash and fold, juggle, or sew into your doll's clothes. So much doll clothes to sew! So many ideas to make into a hat or a pair of pants or a quilt or to throw in your salad. Just add a little of this and a little of that. Fantastic darling!

How is it that people don't know what to do? I think it's perfectly organized here, but some people say this is a bit of a "disarray."

Do you see how many pairs of socks I have? And how many ways I can tie my pony tails? Afro puffs, braided ponytails, twisted ponytails, straightened ponytails. Ribbons in my hair, feathers in my hair, barrettes. I don't need anyone telling me what to do! Thank you very much! I have a perfect un-handle on everything here!

I have three poems I've written over there, and five songs I've written over here, and 1 one blueberry pie, and one apple pie, and one apple turnover (it's different, you know), ...and fresh whipped cream, and one slice of rum cake, and one piece of pound cake, ...and my Grandma's cinnamon sugar toast—annnnnnd I am getting a brand new pair of rollerskates!

VIOLA purses her lips and pretends to flip her hair proudly.

They are going to be pink and gold, or rainbow, and I am going to ride them allllllllll the way to the beach where I will sit in the sun all day, and sing my five songs and three poems, and eat a slice of my blueberry pie with fresh blueberries that I picked, and apple pie, and have three bites of my apple turnover ...with fresh whipped cream. And afterwards, I am going to put on my new socks and a swirly skirt and tie my hair in three ponytails and drink tea while I blow bubbles and chew my gum like my aunties—making it snap over and over between my teeth. How do they do that??

And while I'm skating home, I will find a brand, new, amazing diary to write in. One where I can tell everyone exactly what I am thinking, whether they like it or not! And I will strut and kick my legs and do the twist and listen to"When I Take my Sugar to Tea," while I have my tea party and then I will daydream about all the boys that will fall in love with me. How sweet they will be, and how much fun we will have together, and how my heart will beat so, so, so fast when we kiss. Ah!

Yes, there are more than enough dreams and ideas for me. I don't know WHY my mother thinks her ideas are better than mine! Pah! She should actually be helping me to put all my ideas together. Duh!

There's lots of work to do here! Doesn't she know? I have lots of plans, lots to sing, and lots to write. Plus, the world needs me! Hello! And she's telling me to eat my brussel sprouts?? And finish everything on my plate?

VIOLA widens her eyes looking at the audience pursing her lips.

Well, good thing she's not here right now. I can just finish this drawing before dinner and then I can make more ideas until it's time to get up again tomorrow.

Blackout.

APERTURE

Wide open wide
Wild, nothing planned
Loving you is full of surprise
And shock and terror
And blood and tears

Wide open wide
Scared and panting
Worried and exhausted
Can't focus
Loving you is full of surprise
And laughter and more laughter
Frustration and impatience

So much stretching

                              So wide

So much stretching

                              Heart split

I might be lost

                            Afraid I am lost
                              Where am I?

I might be gone

                              I must be gone

I might be
Pulled apart

                              Still searching

Heart split

                              Wide open
                              so wide

A CRY & A WAIL

Despite the fact that we fill our days with school, work, books, music, relationships, and personal interests, it still feels like something *"special"* is supposed to make our lives begin. What's it going to feel like when life really kicks off? Is it going to start with a Count Basie crescendo, or a Billie Holiday moan? Is it going to be a Stevie Wonder drum fill, or Whitney Houston belting a lonnnnnnnggg long note?

I always thought my life would start with a big bang, like James Brown exclaiming, "Huh! Hit me!" Because of the world of nationally and internationally recognized artists, who I grew up surrounded by, I thought the start of life had to look like a dance scene from a big band opening number like the Nicholas Brothers—full of excitement, tossing bodies, cameras panning, passion, laughter, a little wildness, and something cheeky too like Josephine Baker. But *my life* didn't really "start" with a big bang, instead, it opened with a cry and a wail. The sound of a little baby's voice and my confusion and disorientation at her larger-than-life presence. An *entirely* new chapter in my life *started* with the birth of my daughter.

I found out I was pregnant when one day I realized I hadn't gotten my period for a month and noticed that my appetite had been more voracious than normal. Plus, my boobs were huge! At the time I gave birth to my daughter, we were still living in Brooklyn. I had gone into labor while cleaning the bathroom in our Downtown Brooklyn apartment. Scrubbing floors and wiping the sink and other surfaces in that dark green low light bathroom was like the scene change to this new act in my life.

I had been having false contractions for a few days, so I assumed that's what was happening. After a while, however, I noticed the contractions that were squeezing my lower abdomen hadn't subsided like in the days prior, and this time it must be the real thing. I was in official labor. I realized that cleaning should probably wait. I ought to focus my attention on relaxing my body, to try and practice the HypnoBirthing techniques my husband and I had learned during pregnancy. But it was too late. By the time we made it to the taxi, I was kicking the dividing wall between us and the driver with each contraction, as if I was re-enacting the movements of my child growing inside me.

Riding in the rain to Brooklyn Birthing Center, I felt taken over, almost possessed by a force out of my control. My close friend, Kate, by then a registered nurse, and my husband, Nikolai, were the only other people at the birthing center, along with the midwife and her assistant. I had a reasonably short labor of around thirteen or fourteen hours, but during that time, I was transported to outer dimensions. I lost track of time and forgot about composure as I fully experienced that my body had a mind of its own. My mother had flown in from San Diego and walked into the birthing room just as my daughter, Luna, was entering the world.

From the beginning, Luna's nature was quite the opposite of her name's meaning, and more like the day she arrived—March 21st, the first day of spring. Enter Luna, a petite crocus, premature in size, though full-term, with fair skin, sparse black hair, and a big voice. Like spring, Luna entered with energy, ready to sprout, and challenged everyone around her.

It took several months for my daughter to put on weight. At first, her little body was so tiny that even her skin hung like clothes, uncertain where to fit. But with a few months of regular nuzzling and feasting on breast milk, she grew into herself. Eyes wandering, limbs mobilizing. Her skin was soft, and muscles toned, even as a baby. Though unable to stand for months, she pushed and pushed until she achieved her goal. She had elongated eyes and enviable eyelashes that seemed to look like great, big feathers painted on her little face while she slept.

A true Aries, Luna was physically busy and significantly physically intelligent from the start. Shifting like the tides of the ocean she wanted to climb, push, walk, run, dance and try new things all the time. Although she was built for sports, she never allowed us to sign her up for any for very long, as she objected to rules and adults interrupting play.

Yet, from an early age, she was also incredibly kind. One might not think that of a firecracker, but she has always had a very firm sense of justice and will defend any friend, human, or animal whom she loves. Always good with younger children, even when in preschool herself, the teachers would call on Luna for assistance when kids were upset and unable to be consoled. Luna would appear with her short, stocky body and reckless curls to calmly tend to the crying toddler—somehow able to reassure them that *everything would be alright*. Like her father she has the ability to see multiple perspectives; and perhaps like me, the sensitivity to feel others' feelings. In this way she is like the moon.

But like a comet Luna arrived grabbing enough to fuel herself, and rearranging all that I thought was best for me. For anyone who has birthed a child, or raised a child from infancy, you know that it's a particular voyage with sleep and emotion. The first day that I had Luna, I was incredibly stunned that this little person was here to stay. With us? In our house? My husband and I wondered, "Is she a rental? Where are her parents?," but we quickly realized that we were the ones in charge of this baby bundle. She was ours.

My husband's brother, Dimitri, and our close friend, Ruomi, along with my mother and Kate, were there at the Birthing Center to celebrate Luna's arrival. Soon after, we returned to our apartment on Hoyt Street in Downtown Brooklyn. It was a large, loft-like apartment right in the heart of parking lots, department stores, and street stands. I was completely exhausted but didn't have the words to express what I needed—some quiet and some sleep. I was overwhelmed by the speed of everything.

Looking back, I now realize I just needed someone to know what a first-time mother needs—sleep, food, more sleep, reassurance, a back rub, and more food. I needed temporary remedies to quell the concoction of fears, fatigue and loneliness I was starting to feel. The food we got, but sleep and calm were not on the menu. Luna came home with us, and so did our loving entourage. As a result, we received some much-appreciated assistance with caring for her in the first few hours of her life, but I never had the chance to restore my exhaustion from labor and assess my new job title. Instead, I was launched into motherhood.

Even if you plan it, read books, and go to talks, and doctors, and mom's groups—even if you monitor your cycle like a hawk, logging every variation into the best fertility tracking app, taking every supplement, or planning every aspect of your birth—you still have no control, and no clue what you are in for. No! Clue! I guess you could say that we knew there was no way to fully prepare because we did none of the former. We made no big plans. The only big plan that my husband wisely engineered was to buy us an apartment. That was, and still is, a foundation we firmly stand upon. However, other than that, each move, coo, and cry coming from Luna's little body was a surprise—waking us, worrying us, reminding us, exciting, and shaping us. A little girl who we didn't know but were going to help grow. Although she was the one doing the growing, we were being reconfigured into parents too. That was the real beginning. Everything I thought I was preparing for, she made into an adjustment, like a teacher marking your homework with red-inked comments.

At first Luna's presence forced me to slow down, eliminating any extra, distracting activities, requiring me to focus solely on her; but diapers and baby food can become boring after a while. Ask any parent. So, I would try to fit in extra activities of my own choosing like a long walk or window shopping, but that ended up zapping what little vigor I had. Nursing and caring for an infant are surprisingly energy-consuming, but of course I thought I could manage it like any other task.

As Luna grew, she forced me to speed up, to catch her fast moving body, bounding through the playground and apartment. When she was up and ready—hold on, because she had energy and determination.

Some of this she must have inherited from my husband, who enjoyed nothing more than playing soccer growing up—all he needed was a ball and friends to be content. By the time Luna was a toddler attending preschool, my husband and I were living in our one-bedroom studio. Luna would literally climb the walls as I tried to keep up with meals, playtime, naptime, and everyone's bathroom needs, plus regular house duties. Thankfully, I had a supportive and committed partner.

Luna reaching age three was a milestone, and a highlight in my time as a mom. For the first time, I felt as if I was finally catching up with myself and the first years of parenthood. From infancy to a crawling baby, from a walking babbling baby to then a talking toddler, I started to appreciate my husband's and my fortitude, and I could feel that this little person and I had logged some time together. We had found a rhythm. We had made it this far as a family. Maybe we could do it after all.

Our family began to expand when Luna started preschool at My Little Village on the Lower East Side. That was where she met some of her closest friends and their parents, who became close friends of our's as well. Finding the peer connection, not only for her, but for us as parents, brought an incredible sense of harmony to our household. Not to mention the endless fun it was to watch our kids grow up together as they began discovering the world around them and bloomed into their personalities.

Luna was a fireball of energy—that I was starting to understand. I also secretly liked her toughness. She was a bruiser. Sometimes I wished she would allow herself a little space for tears, though—like when she would fall, face first, at the playground and immediately jump up and start running. My friends would look at me, shocked and worried as I would shrug my shoulders and say, "I know." There was no stopping her. Dwelling on a fall would only make her angry. I watched Luna and she reflected back to me what was and wasn't working in my life.

I started to worry when, as a young girl, Luna began saying that she wished her hair were straight. If there was one thing I felt strongly about when it came to raising a Black girl with a white father, it was that I wanted her to feel comfortably connected to her heritage as a Black woman. With all the love and support that we received from my husband's parents, that was something they couldn't provide. My family wasn't often able to spend long amounts of time with us, for a variety of reasons. I realized that I needed to make a significant change to our world, and fast.

I knew what it felt like to be one of three brown children in a predominantly white space—how tiring and isolating it was not to have your life experience echoed in the world around you. I also knew how relaxing and reassuring it felt when I was surrounded by Black and brown people, our stories, and culture. Through no fault of her own, Luna wasn't seeing enough of herself and her natural beauty, and it was becoming apparent. So, I began intentionally building community and connection that would build her up.

I spent months searching the internet to find animation that starred Black protagonists. At the time, there weren't many options. TV series, such as *Word Girl*, hadn't yet come out, and it would be several years before Black centered movies and tv series like *The Princess and the Frog* and *Boondocks* would arrive. But *Kirikou* started as a favorite. I read her Native American folk tales, tales from all over Africa, selected by Nelson Mandela[32], and I took her to West African music concerts at the Brooklyn Museum. I regularly praised her beauty and natural hair, and my husband and I pointed out when tv shows and media featured white casts, with white boys as lead characters, and why they failed to showcase Black families, or mixed families like ours. We also kept her in public school where we knew she would see versions of herself in her peers and teachers. In a short time, I noticed a shift in Luna's attitude towards her Black identity and of course hair!

It would have been easier, at times, not to highlight Black culture, but the cost to her self-confidence, and perhaps self-love, wasn't something I was willing to risk. I had seen it happen for many biracial chil-

---

32   Mandela, Nelson. *Nelson Mandela's Favorite African Folktales.* (Washington, DC: National Geographic Books, 2007.)

dren. It all became worth it when one day, while washing my hair in the shower (by now Luna was in elementary school), Luna reached up, moving her little fingers through my hair, and exclaimed, "I wish my hair was like yours!" I felt my heart explode with joy. That was when I knew we had beat the system, so to speak—the toxic "If you're white, you're right" mindset. This was a far cry from the little brown girl who had said she wanted straight blonde hair not long before.

Just like all the daily routines we had worked so hard to make feel effortless—like healthy dinners and learning violin—my husband's and my consistent nurturing of Luna's Blackness had also finally settled and was making a positive impact, even against the backdrop of a deeply anti-Black society. When Luna made that comment to me in the shower, I realized that the lens had shifted for her. From that moment on, I noticed Luna enjoying her natural hair. She started to appreciate all the times someone on the street would stop to say how beautiful her curls were which rippled into other areas of her identity. Nurturing Luna to grow as a biracial girl, fully embracing and comfortable in her Blackness, as well as her Austrian and Jewish background, has become one of the many gratifying experiences of raising her.

But the parenting didn't stop there. I also had to look at myself and my own habits—for example, my approach to work. This was probably one of the hardest changes in my life as a parent (and one that I still have to battle at times). At first, I put up a fight—just like a toddler. I wanted to work as I always had. When I had inspiration, I wanted to follow it. Afterall, that's what artists do–they follow their muse. Stop for nothing. If I had emails to write, a show to promote, rehearsals to plan, then I wanted to be able to pursue those things without interruption, the same way I had watched *all the men* (and some women) in music do. But having a baby meant that everything took twice as long. Therefore, I often found myself rushing, and if I was rushing, then Luna became agitated. The rushing never bothered me when I was childless, but once I had a kid, it was like I had a mirror constantly reflecting my behaviors and the values behind them.

Children tend to do what we do, not necessarily what we say. So, I had to clean up a lot of my own habits and face my personal challenges and beliefs as an artist. Like, why was I rushing? Was I afraid all my music opportunities would dissolve if I didn't answer that one email? What did I think would happen if I let myself take a nap instead of working?? It was an ongoing tug of war, but I gradually started to understand that the job requirements for this parent position were entirely different from the requirements of being a musician (or so I thought) and equally, if not more, impactful.

I started to realize that the rules I had placed upon being an artist were crap! They didn't look after me as a person, they looked after music and neglected practically everything else. That didn't feel very spiritually in-tune or innovative, like I wanted my music to be, so I started making changes. It took many years before I recognized that I could only force so much without integrating my personal life and needs into my music practice. Outside of being a hilarious bundle of joy and kisses, and outside of always pushing me to play—Luna reminded me that I could press pause and listen to myself. That there was time to rest, time to just be.

The picture that Luna continues to paint is so much bigger than what I had envisioned for myself. It goes way outside the margins of what I imagined life as a musician and mother could be. Luna has allowed me the pleasure of getting to know her and watch her grow, which—anyone who has a young child in their life can tell you—is an incredibly humbling and inspiring experience. The longer you're in it with them, the more you see the incremental changes, their growth, and your bond as an immense gift. With Luna, I've learned that I am so much more than a musician. As strong as my love is for music, it's best when experienced with her, and now through her, as I watch her grow into a budding singer/songwriter.

I wouldn't trade it for the world! It's been hard, yes! And lonely, but I needed the upgrade. I credit my husband—a big child at heart—with helping to guide us towards such a beautiful and blessed life together.

For all the stubbornness, miscommunication, and bickering—there's nothing like having those two to call home. And at forty-four years old, I have a lot to show for it, and Luna is, by far, the most impressive part of my resume.

LONG SONG

"somebody/ anybody
sing a black girl's song
bring her out
to know herself
to know you
but sing her rhythms
carin/ struggle/ hard times
sing her song of life
she's been dead so long
closed in silence so long
she doesn't know the sound
of her own voice
her infinite beauty
she's half-notes scattered
without rhythm/ no tune
sing her sighs
sing the song of her possibilities
sing a righteous gospel
let her be born
let her be born
& handled warmly[33]"

—NTOZAKE SHANGE

33   Ntozake Shange, *For Colored Girls Who Have Considered Suicide /
      When the Rainbow Is Enu* (New York City: Shameless Hussy Press,
      1975).

Bono State, the Gold Coast, Late morning

1450 near the coast of future Ghana, a young Akan girl plays outside of her home. Her mother is nearby cooking. The smell of fish stew is in the air. There is a comforting breeze before another hot day begins.

AMMA

I don't know why so many of you forget me. I am not a king or a queen or a prince or a princess, I am just a girl. I am Amma, and I'm ten years old. My legs are strong, and Baba says my arms are getting stronger. I can run soooooo far! And so fast! Faster than any boy in my village. And Mama always knows when I am trying to sneak around because she says I have the loudest feet, and the biggest laugh, and no matter what, I can't hide from her. She says that's a good thing because you shouldn't hide who you are.

AMMA wags her finger

Anyway, my mother is the most beautiful woman in the whole world. Her cheeks are so round, and her smile can make anyone happy, Baba says. He says she has magic in her smile. She also has the softest skin, and she smells like sunshine.

I still love to sit in her lap when I'm feeling sad or scared—under the big tree in our village. I love my mama. But sometimes she yells at me because I forget to stir the banku and take it off the fire, and then we have nothing to eat. But it's because I am a child. That's what grand-mother says. She says I am still a child and that is a good thing. "This world needs children and our elders to remember the spirit world. Aunties, mothers, fathers, and even wise men sometimes forget."

Still, I must do the washing, otherwise Mama will beat me and then, when I go with her to market, I will get no yams, only work.

I don't want to miss Mama Akua's fish and yam!

She only brings it once in a while, after many rains. I don't want to miss that. But if you want, you can take my brother and sister. I always tell Mama, "Fine with me! Please take them away!" They are always with me! Always following me and wanting to play. "Amma, come play with me! Amma, help me with my hair! Amma, move over, you are in my way!"

AMMA sucks her teeth.

That is my older brother, Kofi. He is so annoying! I can't wait for him to have a wife and go.

I hope he marries Sibiri. She has the prettiest face and she always brings me presents. Mmm, like the beautiful skirt she gave me that time; and the other time, she came and brought nuts, but only for me! Then Mama made me share it with Sisi and Yawa. Pssst!

Why must there be little brothers and sisters? Mama says it is a good thing because then we will always have a family to care for, and family to care for us. So we will never be lonely. I don't know why this is a good thing. I don't know what it means, but I think I want to be lonely. I only want to run and play with my friends, and go to market with mama, and eat her fufu under the tree, and sit at the water. Look at me jump. No one can beat me!

AMMA begins speaking fearfully as if others can hear her.

Sometimes Baba stays up late talking to himself about white people coming. "What white people?" Mama asks. "You mean Fifi?" And then she makes a worried look because Fifi is not white, he is just born without his real skin. "It's not his fault," she says, and then looks worried because she is afraid that Baba is being taken by spirits.

But I know he is right. One day white people will come. Real white people—not like Fifi. They are not like us; they speak in strange sounds and they are always hungry. Always walking with a frown, and their smell is strange, like old goat's milk.

AMMA crinkles her nose and brow.

These people are not like Fifi. Fifi loves his village. He would never want to hurt anyone here. But these white people—they will take other Babas from their families. There will be screaming and crying. They will be hurting our mothers, burning fires, eating our food, and then spitting on us, calling us dirty. There will be kicking and killing. Killing our animals, killing our trees, taking our stones, taking our plants. Taking mothers, taking fathers. I see them, too. But I don't tell anyone. The white people that Baba speaks of, with their long hair and scared faces. I don't know why they are so scared and angry, but they are. They are red too. So red and hot! What would make them want to travel so far from their home?

Sweating and swollen and burning red. I don't know why, but they will. Things will change. Not for me or my children, but maybe their children.

I would never want to leave my home. There is so much fun here.

In our village there are so many people. I have so many friends to play with. And Mama? She has soooo many friends to talk with that Baba says we need to move because she will never make dinner on time if she is always talking and laughing and making jokes. But she says that is how dinner gets made! He must stick to man things, and she will stick to Mama things. That always makes Baba stop talking.

If it weren't for all my aunties, Sisi would not be here too. Mama Yaba was there when Mama was pouring life out, like a pot of banku and stew. I was so scared. I had to keep getting her water and wiping her face, but she was crying and sweating, and Baba couldn't make it better. It wasn't until Mama Yaba placed her hands all the way inside Mama and turned Sisi, that Sisi could come out. And just like how he is now, he came out complaining. I didn't say anything, but I thought, "How are you crying after all that you did to Mama? You should be thanking her!" And all she did was hug him and kiss him while my aunties sang. "Why does Sisi get a song for hurting Mama?" I thought. I still don't think it is right.

Just in my family alone, I have soooo many aunties and uncles, and Grandmother is still alive. We go to see her every Saturday. But it is really too much—oh? I love Grandmother, but Mama forgets that is when Afi and I must meet. Afi is my best friend. She and I met before we were born—that is what our mothers say, because they were both big with bellies and neither of them could stop eating fufu. That is how they knew that we would be friends. Afi and I love to go play by the water and pretend to be fisherwomen—catching fish, cutting off their heads, and selling them at the market before we come home to cook for our husbands and children. We also talk to the spirits of the forest. That is where I learned to see, not just what's in front of me, but through. Afi doesn't know that I can hear the spirits when we talk to them. She just thinks I am pretending like her. But it doesn't matter. I like having her there with me. She is a good friend. She always remembers my birthday, and I always remember to make her laugh when she is feeling sad.

And I love my grandmother. Even though she is old, so old that her face looks like the outside of a cassava,

AMMA covers her mouth quickly

but her laugh is sooo loud and high as a monkey. Whenever she laughs, her face wrinkles so that her eyes almost disappear. But it makes everyone happy, too. Mama says that is what laughter should do. It should spread like the river. She says I get my laugh from Grandmother, and I should share it with pride, because Grandmother won't be here forever. And it doesn't matter if I am not good at hiding—even when I try to sneak around, I always stand out.

You see, you must remember that we are here now. No king or queen, no prince or princess. Just me and Sisi and Yawa...and Kofi. Psst! You can't forget us. Look how many of us there are.

Lights fade

GLASS CEILING

Bushwick, Brooklyn, 10 AM

A young adult woman in her late twenties sits at the edge of her bed in a pair of overalls. Her afro is pulled back into a ponytail. There is a bed against one wall with a bookshelf full of Black feminist books on one side and a yoga mat and blocks on the other. A small desk with her laptop is placed on the opposite wall. Next to her desk sits a small keyboard in the corner near a window with several plants. Sheets of music and writing rest on the keyboard. There is a large skylight overhead.

MELODY

I just fell in...finally! The sun broke through, or maybe I woke up on the right side of the bed, or had the right combination of vegetables or protein, or drank enough water—I don't know. Whatever it was I just decided to take a chance, close my eyes...feel again!

I can hear myself

MELODY says to herself

And escape.

Everyone else's thoughts and murmurs and guilt and pride and anger...and sadness. It just Stopped.

All those doubts. All the questions and to-do lists and "should I?"
"shouldn't I?" Ugh!
All those detours!
I could actually hear myself!

It's like silence, actually...Singing.
You hear the music outside, but inside...it's like silence.

Or one long hum. Yea, one eternal hum that everyone keeps adding to
and generating over and over. From your great-great-grandmother to
your uncle on your mother's side to, you know, your second Cousin
twice removed to that woman across the street who never talks to you
(even tho' she sees You!)

It's like silence.

No one else's impressions
No sizing you up
No measuring myself against...

I can hear myself

   MELODY pauses to listen and smiles

I like it
Just like that, back-to-back. One song after the next.
One song, then the next, then the next
No one's expectations
Not even your own

The problem is...I still get caught. You know? Caught in the briar
patch. Caught forgetting that I already have the answer.

I mean I'm *sooo* smart I learned how to use music to not only free myself but also trap myself and then free myself again!

MELODY shakes her head as she begins watering plants

Isn't that crazy?

This country.
The way it gets under your skin and your nails
Til you're scrubbing and washing and trying to remove parts of you
that have no business being removed.
Amazing, how we can have the key and forget to use it...and then when
we do, use it against ourselves.

MELODY stops watering and just looks out the window

You know when you step outside there's a whooollle lot more! Like, A
LOT more! More than *they* tell us.

Waaaay more to see. Like there are levels! You think you broke
through and then there's another glass ceiling, and another.

Ah! I can hear myself

I can love myself
I can hear myself

One song after the next
Just singing a simple song.

Your own little jukebox
Or church
Your own peace of mind

Sometimes I wonder if this is what Jimi Hendrix felt like when he was off transporting himself to other dimensions. Like just dee ne nee nee...

MELODY begins mimicking playing a guitar

Sometimes I wonder
Is this what rapture feels like?

Black out

FALL INTO YOU

I want to Fall into you, music
Back in your arms
The world gets too hard
Full of straight lines, straight thinkers
Rulers and hard edges
It forgets itself
I want to Fall into you
Held again
Fully expanded
Every version of myself
I want to Fall into you
Back inside myself
Back home
Back together again
The best fairytale
I want to Fall into you, music
My mind Free
Boundless
Only God

EPILOGUE

Years ago, I had the pleasure of working with a wonderful actress in a series of short plays. After rehearsal one day, she and I started talking about the challenges of art-making. We both agreed it wasn't so much the performing we struggled with, but more the returning to regular life after the figurative curtain had closed. It was then we most often encountered the shadows of our minds. Our fears of the future, when the next gig was going to come, challenges with time management, relationships, concerns about paying the bills, and self-doubt. Being onstage, on the other hand, was quite easy—that was the fun part. There, we could surrender all the big *life* stuff and easily fall into what was happening in the scene or music. That's when I came to realize what all the training and preparation is actually for.

Ever since I was little, I had a burning desire to become a successful, well-known singer—writing and performing my music around the world. However, most art schools don't fully instruct you as to how to put together your day-to-day life in order to accomplish this. The balance between life and art is hard! Yet, the older I get, the more aware I am of how important it is that I connect with myself and others through music. Despite the years of art and life failures and successes, that connection has only strengthened. It's where I know I can genuinely and fully express myself. As a result, I have even more appreciation for my performing practice.

Since that conversation, I started to rethink my ideas and impetus for making art—why it's here and what we ought to use it for. In addition to any individual's personal message or idea they're seeking to convey, I would argue the gift of art is not always what it gives us as performers, but what it gives us as people. As a mother, wife, friend, mentor, and performer—music and performance offer me a model for how to be in the world. How can I be as interested, enthusiastic, calm, and appreciative as when I'm singing? How can I listen to others as fully as I listen when I'm making music? How can I be as supportive and nurturing to my body, my energy, and other people, as I am when I have to sing? If the music was supposed to end onstage, then how do we explain the depth of our passion for it? There are details in the making of music that allow us to be better humans—if we fully open ourselves to art's wisdom.

ACKNOWLEDGEMENTS

I am so grateful to have been able to write this book over the last few years. First I want to acknowledge Nikki Starcat Shields and The Sacred Path writers group where I workshopped nearly every piece included in this book. Thank you to my beta readers, starting with Madeline Murray, and followed by Hjordis Linn-Blanford, Don Blanford, Valborg Fletre-Linn, Lee Stern, Nikolai Moderbacher, Alicia Hines, and Tendayi Kuumba.

Thank you to Marika Hughes and the Looking Glass friends and family week where I was able to parcel out steps for beginning the editing process and also break bread with fellow sister artists. Thank you to Jen Shyu's online artist community and Ayelet Rose-Gottlieb and the Orchard of Pomegranates where I received so much support and inspiration to continue to envision new ways of creating art that honor all parts of me.

Thank you to my dear friend Sibyl Rolle, whose endless conversations about life, love, sisterhood, music, and Blackness, were crucial to the completion of this book and my overall confidence in releasing it.

Thank you to my brother-from-another-mother Ruomi for believing in me and encouraging me with this project.

Thank you to Jessica Kaloutas for our weekly accountability calls around all things life, business, mamahood, healing and luxury:) which have made the weeks so much easier to surrender to.

Thank you to my friend Kate for your visionary eyes and always being there to look over artwork and visuals. Thank you to my mother-in-law Eileen Moderbacher for bringing her graphic design superpowers. Thank you Whitney Austin for her wonderful painting which I commissioned for the front cover!

Finally, thank you to Lindsey, Andrw, and Lucy—the team at Get It Done for making the process of putting together this book such an encouraging and smooth one. Thank you to April Reigart, my editor. I couldn't have imagined someone more aligned for the job! Thank you to Lai-Lin for continuously working your magic and thoughtfulness around all aspects of the release of this book and my private studio.

And of course, thank you to my mom, Kristen, Nikolai, Luna, and anyone else who was willing to respond to my random text messages and voice notes with urgent questions about titles, sentence structure, and settings. I am so grateful to all of you. Thank you to my dad who has been quite excited about the release of this book. And to my students, thank you for always trusting me and teaching me.

BIOGRAPHY

Pyeng Threadgill is an American vocalist, songwriter, writer, and video artist, as well as a voice and movement teacher. As a vocalist/performer, she creates what she calls New Porch Music, a form based on the traditions of Black American folk, soul, jazz, and improvisational music. She uses these traditions to create connected conversations whereby audiences may reflect on their own life stories and identities for healing and empowerment.

In her fourth solo album and multimedia project, entitled *Head Full of Hair, Heart Full of Song*, Ms. Threadgill shines a light on hair, adornment, ancestry, and the political, as well as spiritual implications of race, hair, and identity. She sees this album as a digital talisman for young Black women, girls and non-binary adolescents to use as they move through the world.

Prior to the release of *Head Full of Hair, Heart Full of Song*, Ms. Threadgill began researching the frightful circumstances of climate change, unearthing a new song cycle, *Songlines. Songlines: Singing The Land* explores the foundational contributions of African and Indigenous people to food justice and sustainability movements.

In 2008, Pyeng was awarded a fellowship in music composition from New York Foundation for The Arts for her third solo album, *Portholes to a Love & Other Short Stories. Portholes to a Love* traverses concepts of reality and magic, humanity and nature, as shared in the short stories of renowned authors. Taking inspiration from writers such as Isabelle Allende, Jamaica Kincaid, Jhumpa Lahiri, and others, Pyeng absorbs their words to convey the love, pain, and longing of being human.

With her two first albums *Sweet Home: The Music of Robert Johnson* and *Of the Air*, Threadgill began to tour both nationally and internationally, headlining music venues and festivals around the globe. She has performed at Montreal Jazz Festival, Atlanta Jazz Festival, Yoshi's San Francisco, Banlieues Bleues, Cognac Blues Festival, The Sunset Sunside Jazz Club, Blue Note Late Night Series, Clifford Brown Jazz Festival, Jazz Standard, The Iridium, Detroit Institute for the Arts, San Sebastian Jazz Festival, Earshot Jazz Festival, Scullers, Half Note Jazz Club in Greece, as well as iconoclast downtown New York venues, such as Rockwood Music Hall, and Nublu.

In 2007, Pyeng was a featured artist in the music documentary *Retour A Goree,* starring Senegalese vocalist/composer, Youssou N'Dour. She later appeared at Montreux Jazz Festival with this project. As a guest artist, Pyeng has appeared with Amina Claudine Myers' Generations 4, Marc Cary, Urban Bush Women, hattie gossett, Contra Tiempo, and others. She has been featured by the mayor's office on New York one. In 2023, Ms. Threadgill became a recipient of a grant from the Jerome Foundation. *Lost & Found: Finding the Power in Your Voice* is Pyeng's first book.

To find out how to work with Pyeng, or learn about her next performance, workshop, talk, or offering, visit:
http://pyengnyc.com

BIBLIOGRAPHY

Alvarez, Ana María, and César. *Full Still Hungry.* Contra Tiempo et al. Performance New York, NY, 2011.

Alvarez, César. "Futurity." *Futurity.* (New York: Theatre Communications Group, 2017.)

Borgeaud, Pierre-Yves. *Retour à Gorée.* Axiom Films, 2007. 112 minutes. https://www.imdb.com/title/tt0798733/

Brown, James. "Say It Loud—I'm Black and I'm Proud." *A Soulful Christmas.* King, 1968.

Camalier, Greg. *Muscle Shoals.* Magnolia Pictures, 2013. 111 minutes. https://www.imdb.com/title/tt2492916/

Casseus, Frantz. "Fi Nan Bois." *Haitiana.* Afro-Carib Records, 1971.

Casseus, Frantz. "Meci Bon Die." *Haitiana.* Afro-Carib Records, 1971.

Cherry, Neneh. "Buffalo Stance." *Raw Like Sushi.* Virgin, 1989.

Encyclopedia.com. N.d. "Firefly." Accessed May 23, 2023. https://www.encyclopedia.com/plants-and-animals/animals/zoology-invertebrates/firefly

En Vogue. "Free Your Mind." *Funky Divas.* Eastwest, 1992.

Fure, Ashley. *Filament.* Performance. New York: David Geffen Hall, 2018.

Fure, Ashley and Adam. *The Force of Things: An Opera for Objects.* Performance. Darmstadt, Germany, 2016.

Houston, Whitney. "How Will I Know." *Whitney Houston. Arista,* 1985

Houston, Whitney. "Saving All My Love For You." *Whitney Houston. Arista,* 1985.

James, Etta . "I'd Rather Go Blind." *Tell Mama.* Cadet, 1968.

Johnson, Robert. "When You Got a Good Friend." *King of the Delta Blues Singers*. Columbia, 1969.

Kimmerer, Robin Wall. *Braiding Sweetgrass* (Minneapolis: Milkweed Editions, 2013.)

King, Emily. "Good Friend." *The Switch*. Making Music, 2015.

Lincoln, Abbey. "Living Room." *People in Me*. Inner City Records, 1978.

Lincoln, Abbey. "Learning How to Listen." *Wholly Earth*. Verve Records, Gitanes Jazz Productions, 1998.

Lindsay, Daniel, and Martin, T.J. *Tina*. HBO, 2021. 118 minutes. https://www.hbo.com/movies/tina

Mandela, Nelson. *Nelson Mandela's Favorite African Folktales*. (Washington, DC: National Geographic Books, 2007.)

Mathieu, W.A. *The Listening Book: Discovering Your Own Music* (Boulder: Shambala Publications, 1991.)

McFerrin, Bobby. "Yes You." *Medicine Music*. 1990.

Mingus, Charles. "Fables of Faubus." *Minus Ah Um. 1959.*

Shange, Ntozake. *For Colored Girls Who Have Considered Suicide / When the Rainbow Is Enu* (New York City: Shameless Hussy Press, 1975).

Threadgill, Pyeng. "Safe and Sound." Portholes To A Love & Other Stories. Stray Dog Music, 2009.

Twenty-Four Italian Songs and Arias. (New York: G. Schirmer, 1948.)

Victor, Fay. "Black Women's Music." Victor, 2021. Accesed May 24, 2023. https://www.fayvictor.com/compositions/black-womens-music-2020/

Wikipedia contributors, "Eroticism," Wikipedia, The Free Encyclopedia, https://en.wikipedia.org/w/index.php?title=Eroticism&oldid=1156225717 (Accessed May 23, 2023).

Wonder, Stevie. "Never Deamed You'd Leave in Summer." *Where I'm Coming From*. Tamla, 1971.

Wonder, Stevie. "The Secret Life of Plants." *Journey Through the Secret Life of Plants*. Motown Records, 1979.

Zollar, Jawole Willa Jo; Carlos, Laurie; gossett, hattie; Harris, Craig. *Shelter.* Urban Bush Women et al. Performance, 1988.

Recommended Listening, Viewing,
and Honorable Mentions

Music

Cliff, Jimmy. "The Harder They Come." *The Harder They Come.* Song. Island, 1972.

Cooke, Sam. "You Send Me." *Sam Cooke.* Song. Keen, 1958.

Franklin, Aretha. *Amazing Grace.* Album. Atlantic, 1972.

Franklin, Aretha. "I Never Loved a Man (The Way I Love You)." *I Never Loved a Man the Way I Love You.* Song. Atlantic, 1967.

Jackson, Mahalia. Writ. Civilla D. Martin. Acc. Duke Ellington. "His Eye Is on the Sparrow." *The Essential Mahalia Jackson.* Song. Columbia, 1980.

Jackson, Michael. prod. Prince. *Off the Wall.* Album. Epic, CBS, 1979.

Khan, Chaka. "Through the Fire." *I Feel for You.* Song. Warner, 1984.

Myers, Amina C. "Have Mercy Upon Us/Chant." *Song for Mother E.* Song. Leo, 1980.

Pickett, Wilson. "Mustang Sally." *The Wicked Pickett.* Song. Atlantic, 1967.

Pleasure, King. *King Pleasure.* Album. Everest Records Archive, 1972.

The Staple Sisters. "I'll Take You There." *Be Altitude: Respect Yourself.* Album. Stax, 1972.

Vaughan, Sarah. "Lullaby of Birdland." *Sarah Vaughan.* Song. EmArcy, 1954.

Film

Lee, Spike, dir. *School Daze.* 1988; Columbia Pictures. Film

Maysles, Albert and David. *Gimme Shelter.* 1970; Maysles Films, Penforta. Documentary Film.

Maysles, Albert and David. *Grey Gardens.* 1975; Portrait Films. Documentary Film.

McGruder, Aaron, creator. *The Boondocks.* 2005-2014. Adult Swim, 2005, Animated Television Series.

Musker, John, dir. *The Princess and the Frog.* 2009; Walt Disney Studios.

Ocelot, Michel, dir. *Kirikou and the Sorceress.* 1998; Gébéka Films.

SanAngelo, David, dir. *WordGirl.* 2007-2015. PBS Kids, 2007, Animated Television Series.

Satterfield, Stephen. *High on the Hog.* 2021; Netflix. Documentary Series.

Printed in the USA
CPSIA information can be obtained
at www.ICGtesting.com
LVHW052001171023
761403LV00003B/4

9 781956 989311